The Quilt

Each year, The Addict's Mom community creates a quilt to be displayed at the FED UP! Rally in Washington, DC. Members of TAM create squares to represent the loved ones in their lives who have struggled with addiction. The color of each square has a specific meaning:

- **Red** symbolizes a loved one in active addiction.

- **Gray** symbolizes a loved one currently incarcerated as a result of their addiction.

- **Black** symbolizes a loved one who has lost their life to addiction.

- **White** symbolizes a loved one in recovery.

The finished quilt serves as a striking representation of only a small portion of the thousands of families affected by addiction each year.

Praise for *Without Shame*

In the pages of *Without Shame,* Barbara Theodosiou stitches together her family's stories of pain and healing—a patchwork of scars and mending hearts. Sharing patterns and perspectives, thoughts and feelings, her words wrap like an old quilt around the shoulders of other moms with addicted children, with the powerful warmth of truth and strength.

—Sandra Swenson, author of *Tending Dandelions* and *The Joey Song*

Millions of mothers struggle silently with an addicted son or daughter. In *Without Shame,* a candid account of the impact of addiction, Barbara pierces both silence and shame, and helps mothers know where to turn.

—D'Anne Burwell, author of *Saving Jake: When Addiction Hits Home*

The heartbreakingly familiar story of the devastation of addiction told by the pioneer of online family support.

—Maureen Cavanagh, author of *If You Love Me:*
A Mother's Journey Through Her Daughter's Addiction and Recovery

I am so grateful for Barbara's courage to begin The Addict's Mom (TAM) and to share her story. I also share my journey publicly, and I don't think I could have done that without being able to share without shame in TAM. Thank you, Barbara, for being a changemaker in a world afraid of change.

—Katie Donovan, Founder and CEO of A Mother's Addiction Journey

Barbara's generosity and compassion have resulted in a following of more than 100,000 moms with children lost, those still struggling, and those recovered. She was always ahead of the curve when it came to understanding that stigma must go, and her willingness to be honest at great personal sacrifice in a culture of shame will always be remembered, appreciated, and admired.

—Beverly Buncher, founder and CEO of the
BALM Training Institute for Family Recovery Services
and author of *BALM: The Loving Path to Family Recovery*

Like Theodosiou's organization, The Addict's Mom, this book will be a source of insight, comfort, and support for anyone impacted by a loved one's addiction, assuring readers that they are not alone.

—Beverly Conyers, author of *Addict in the Family*

without shame

The Addict's Mom and Her Family
Share Their Stories of Pain and Healing

BARBARA THEODOSIOU

with the editors at Hazelden Publishing

Hazelden Publishing
Center City, Minnesota 55012
hazelden.org/bookstore

Names: Theodosiou, Barbara, 1959- author.
Title: Without shame : the addict's mom and her family share their stories of pain
    and healing / Barbara Theodosiou ; with the editors at Hazelden Publishing.
Description: Center City, Minnesota : Hazelden Publishing, [2020] |
Identifiers: LCCN 2019041843 (print) | LCCN 2019041844 (ebook) |
    ISBN 9781616497798 | ISBN 9781616497804 (epub)
Subjects: LCSH: Drug abuse--United States. | Drug addicts--United States--Family
    relationships.
Classification: LCC HV5825 .T53 2020 (print) | LCC HV5825 (ebook) |
    DDC 362.29/13--dc23
LC record available at https://lccn.loc.gov/2019041843
LC ebook record available at https://lccn.loc.gov/2019041844

Editor's notes

This publication is not intended as a substitute for the advice of health care professionals.

Some names, details, and circumstances have been omitted or changed to protect the privacy of those mentioned in this publication.

Readers should be aware that websites listed in this work may have changed or disappeared between when this work was written and when it is read.

24 23 22 21 20   1 2 3 4 5 6

Cover design: Terri Kinne
Quilt photography: Brad Hadsall
Photo insert pages: Images courtesy of the Theodosiou family unless otherwise noted
Developmental editor: Heather Silsbee
Editorial project manager: Jean Cook

■ ■ ■

This book is dedicated to

Rudy, who has stood by my side through everything

Fred, who taught me the true value of family

and my beautiful children, Peter, Daniel, Nicole,
and Alex, who remind me every day that my life
has been full of blessings

Contents

Editors' Note

Addiction is a family disease. If you have experience with addiction your-self, have loved ones who live with addiction, or have read other recov-ery narratives, you have probably heard that phrase. What does it really mean? For one answer, you can look at numbers. For example, a Pew Research Center survey conducted in August 2017 found that 46 percent of Americans say they have a family member or close friend who is or has been addicted to drugs.* Those numbers, of course, don't represent the many additional Americans who may not yet be aware that they belong to this group.

The more comprehensive answer is much more subjective, and each person may have a different answer. "Addiction is a family disease" means that it's impossible for addiction to live in a vacuum. Every person who lives, or has lived, with an addiction touches countless other lives. When they touch other lives, they bring with them all of the wonderful, brilliant, and unique qualities that they have had since long before their addiction took hold. They also bring all of the horrors that their disease has brought into their lives. Anyone who loves and cares for a person with an addiction experiences all of these terrifying, enlightening, destructive, and beautiful qualities at the same time. The image of the person they knew before the disease clashes with the behaviors they are now forced to confront. Everyone involved in the equation, whether they are friends, parents, grandparents, partners, siblings, or classmates—whether they are biologically or legally related or not—is faced with an impossible question: How can I continue to love and care about this person who

---

* John Gramlich, "Nearly half of Americans have a family member or close friend who's been addicted to drugs," Pew Research Center, October 26, 2017, https://www.pewresearch.org/fact-tank/2017/10/26/nearly-half-of-americans-have-a-family-member-or-close-friend-whos-been-addicted-to-drugs/.

is so important to me, and also love and care for myself? Is that balance even possible to achieve? The dynamics that emerge are always complex and nuanced—and often ugly, heartbreaking, and misunderstood.

There is another way in which addiction doesn't exist in a vacuum. Like many diseases, the history of the diagnosis, causes, effects, and understanding of addiction is long, complicated, sometimes contradictory, and very much still ongoing. If you're interested in those histories, theories, and ongoing developments, there are many excellent books, films, articles, and other resources for you to explore. A few of them are mentioned in the Recommended Resources section at the back of this book. This book is not an exploration of that history, but it is an example of it. It does explore one of the common themes that you'll see emerge from many, if not all, of those other texts. When addiction develops in a person, it is almost always accompanied by a host of other complicating factors in that person's history. To give an incomplete list, addiction to a substance is very often accompanied or preceded by mental health disorders, other addictive behaviors, physical or emotional abuse, traumatic events, unhealthy relationships, divorce, poverty, homelessness, marginalization, or a long family history of other addictions, whether or not those addictions were recognized or acknowledged at the time they occurred. Often, it's difficult to identify when the effects of one of these factors ends and another begins, and people may argue whether attempting to distinguish between them is even a worthy exercise. Several of these factors exist in the stories of Barbara Theodosiou and her family. Their stories are about addiction and everything that accompanies it, both positive and negative, both before and after it entered their lives.

In the midst of our current addiction epidemic, a lot of brave people have come forward to share their stories. These people are brave because our past is full of communities and individuals who have been publicly shamed, incarcerated, pushed out of their jobs and homes, or denied medical help because of their experience with addiction. Many people still fall victim to this treatment. Regardless, every day people come forward to share their stories on social media, on personal blogs, in documentaries and feature films, and on national news. Some share their stories in books. One thing you will notice about this book is that, unlike many more traditional memoirs, it contains more than one voice and more than one story. To say addiction is a family disease presupposes that each person affected by that disease is an individual with unique experiences, needs, genetics, feelings, and voices. Their stories sometimes overlap and sometimes contradict each other, but each of those individuals affects all of the others. This book is an attempt to capture a picture of what that dynamic looks like for one family.

To paint a realistic portrait of addiction, we have to let the people affected use the words that make the most sense to them. Admittedly, this is one of the more challenging aspects of editing any biographical work, but also one of the most crucial. Everyone involved in this project has done their best to make sure the words used accurately reflect the speaker's feelings and are as sensitive as possible to the experiences of anyone reading them. We have also made the conscious choice to use some loaded words and ideas that may not resonate with everyone and may even offend some readers. One of those words, "addict," is even in the subtitle of this book. This word, along with many others associated with addiction, mental health, and trauma, carries a lot of historical baggage and stigma. It is often used as a cruel attempt to reduce a person down to a stereotype and argue that they deserve lesser treatment. Because of this, some people wisely choose not to use the word "addict" at all, pointing out the incredible pain it can cause for anyone who has been labeled with it against their will. Others, however, fully aware of that baggage and risk, proudly claim it as their own, in an attempt to unabashedly represent everything they and their loved ones have fought for and against. From listening to their words, we hope you will come to know that when Barbara, her family, and countless others directly affected by addiction use these terms for themselves and those they love, they are attempting to reduce stigma, not amplify it.

The stories presented here are true and accurate to the knowledge of those who are presenting them. Some names and details have been omitted to protect the privacy of those involved. Some details have been changed or omitted because memory is imperfect, especially when those memories are linked to traumatic events.

Whatever your situation, we hope you see a part of yourself and your experience in these pages. Even if you have not been touched by addiction personally, it's likely you will find something that hits close to home. We hope these stories prove to you that you're not alone.

— The editors at Hazelden Publishing

without shame

CHAPTER 1

Becoming an Addict's Mom

It was 2008 when I got the call from Daniel's high school secretary. He was sixteen and the school called me to say, "We think your son is on drugs." My immediate thought was "There's no way." From when they were little, I told my kids everything I knew about the dangers of drugs, and I thought I knew a lot. I taught them all the catchy takeaways to remember, like "First the man takes the drug, then the drug takes the drug, then the drug takes the man" and "One is too many, and one thousand is never enough." And I was very open with them about an uncle of theirs who had been addicted to heroin. I told them that, even though their uncle is doing well now, everything he went through was horrible both for him and everyone in our family. And I made it clear that, because of their family history, they were at a greater risk of becoming addicted themselves. I couldn't believe Daniel would take that risk.

Then again, it wasn't like there weren't any signs. There was the time not too long before when Daniel and a friend of his stole alcohol from our liquor cabinet and his dad had to pick him up passed out in front of the local movie theater. And we had suspected there was something wrong with him the last couple of weeks. Either my husband, Rudy, or I would take Daniel and his sister, Nicole, to school in the mornings, and Daniel had started getting sick on the rides. He looked really off and a few times asked us to pull the car over and opened the door because he felt like he was going to throw up. I asked what was wrong and if he wanted to stay home, but he would always insist on going. "No, no, I'm fine. It's nothing." He had been getting bullied at school more and more recently, and I thought maybe he was having panic attacks.

The day the school called and I went to pick him up, he was in the middle of a standardized test. It's funny, I remember seeing him sitting there in class when I walked up to the door. He looked up and smiled when he saw me, and I thought he looked so handsome. He was wearing a cute tank top and was in great shape. But when I talked to him, I could tell something was off. I told him I was taking him right away to get drug tested, and he smiled and said, "Okay, but I'm not on anything. Mom, one of these days we're going to laugh about this." That was one of my sayings when the kids got in trouble. One of these days we'll laugh about this, but not today. I called Rudy, who owns his own business, and took Daniel to the clinic where Rudy does drug testing for his employees. The test came back clean. No drug use was detected, and Daniel didn't seem surprised.

But once the idea was planted in my head, I couldn't let it go. Something was clearly wrong, and Daniel was never good at keeping secrets, so I would find out what he was hiding. I called everyone I knew who might have some idea what was going on with him and finally got the answer from my oldest son, Peter, and one of his friends, who talked to Daniel. They told me Daniel was using a drug named dextromethorphan, known to users as DXM, which I had never heard of in my life. It's the active ingredient in some varieties of Robitussin and other over-the-counter cough medicines. When you take a lot, it can give you hallucinations and out-of-body experiences. It can also cause side effects like confusion, nausea, and vomiting. Apparently a lot of the kids at his school were using it, and it doesn't show up on most drug tests, which explains why Daniel didn't seem very concerned about the test.

I was shocked and angry, but honestly, not incredibly concerned. I had never even heard of this drug, so I didn't know the dangers of it, and if it was over-the-counter it couldn't be that bad. At least it wasn't heroin or meth, right? I confronted Daniel and yelled at him, "Daniel, after everything I've told you about your uncle, how could you start doing this? This is not going to happen! You're not using any drugs in this house." I put my foot down and made all the usual threats. He admitted it right away and insisted, "All right already, I get it! I won't do it again!" Of course, he did do it again.

The next time I got a terrible call, it was from the hospital saying he was there being treated for an overdose. Now, I was terrified. I knew what an overdose meant, and my heart skipped a beat. I thought he was dying right then. This problem was bigger than anything I could fix with a stern conversation. Luckily, as far as overdoses go, it could have been a lot worse. He had taken too many Triple Cs (the slang term for Coricidin Cough and Cold tablets) and passed out. Someone had found him and called the ambulance, and he would be okay. For a moment, I almost wished it was heroin he was taking. At least then I would know what I was up against. I knew close to nothing about this drug, and he could just go get it at any corner drugstore. I told him he was going to treatment, but I was not as confident in my decision as I seemed. I realized I didn't know how to get him into addiction treatment. I had no idea who to call or where to send him. I sat glued to my computer at my kitchen table almost constantly for more than a week, looking at a million different possibilities. How in the world was I supposed to pick the right one? But I was getting pressure from Rudy, who insisted Daniel could not stay there and use drugs around us, and especially not around our youngest son, Alex. Finally, I chose a place out of state that took my ex-husband's insurance, and he agreed to take Daniel there.

Daniel seemed okay with our plan and cooperated without much trouble. But after about a week, Daniel called and told me one of the other kids had beaten him up. He pleaded with me, "Mom, everyone hates me. Please get me out of here. I promise I won't do it anymore, just please don't send me away again." I talked to Daniel's father, and he agreed to go pick Daniel up and bring him home. When Daniel got home, he was so upset. He just kept pleading with me, "Please don't ever send me anywhere again, please don't, please don't." Just days later, he overdosed again. This time we found an upscale treatment center nearby that specialized in treatment of co-occurring substance and mental health disorders in youth. It was covered by Daniel's father's insurance, so we decided to send him there.

By that time, I realized I needed help just as much as Daniel did. There was never a lack of people to give me unsolicited opinions. From the beginning, I was open with friends and colleagues about what was happening with Daniel. Plenty of people gave me suggestions on what I should do, or more commonly, what I shouldn't do. I heard that I shouldn't pick him up, I shouldn't buy him anything, I shouldn't call him. People would say that I was ruining his chances if I did this or that. But none of them had addicted children, and everything they said contradicted every motherly instinct I had. They didn't realize that from the moment I found out he was using drugs, I saw Daniel dying in front of me, and I was dying along with him. Some of my good friends did really listen and try to be supportive, but they just couldn't help me. And I couldn't think about anything else, so I wasn't much of a friend to them either.

I went to a couple of meetings of Nar-Anon, a Twelve Step group for people with addicted loved ones. I ended up being the only mother at the meetings I went to. There were cousins and siblings and friends and girlfriends, and I just couldn't handle sitting there quietly listening to their stories. I already knew how it felt to love someone with an addiction. I had experienced it with my brother years ago. I loved him as much as anyone in the world, and I was devastated. But this feeling was different from anything I had ever experienced. I was so raw that I just wanted to yell, "If your boyfriend won't stop using, you can dump him. This is my son!" Sitting at my kitchen table again with my computer, looking for any possible resources that wouldn't make me want to scream, I kept thinking that there had to be other moms doing the exact same thing. They would be the only people who could really understand what was happening, who could really help me. I just didn't know them. My attitude was, if you want to meet someone, you need to create a reason to meet them. If you need something that doesn't exist, you have to create it yourself.

Social media was starting to gain popularity then, and I was using a Facebook page for a women's business group I was managing. Facebook was easy to use and access, so I decided to start a Facebook group to try to find other mothers like me. I got the name of the group from Daniel. He had learned in treatment and meetings that he had to be honest about his issues and admit he was an addict. So, he told me, "That means you're the addict's mom." We chuckled about that a little bit at the time. We had no idea how much those labels would come to define us.

■

Nicole

Hindsight

In hindsight, the first sign I had was an Advil container in our shared bathroom. One time I opened it and noticed that the pills inside looked strange—different from what Advil normally looks like. It was kind of weird, but I didn't think much of it. At that point I had never even heard of someone taking cold pills to get high, you know. I was fourteen, in ninth grade, and Daniel was in tenth grade. At that time, Daniel and I were going to the same school, so either my mom or Rudy would drive us both in the mornings. Daniel started getting sick on the way to school, to the point that a couple of times we had to pull over so he could throw up. That was strange—none of us really knew what was wrong, since he seemed fine otherwise. It still never crossed my mind that he could be using drugs until my mom told me.

I think she found out from the school and told me one day when she was picking me up from dance team practice. Once she told me, all the other elements of his recent behavior kind of clicked in my head. It was a very weird thing for me. I looked up some information on DXM to try to understand what it did and why he was using it, but I didn't really get it. It just wasn't for me.

In the beginning, I never thought that it would become what it became. I knew kids at school used drugs socially at parties, but I never saw it turn into more than that. I never thought my brother was going to become a drug addict. I didn't think it was gonna become this huge thing. I'm thinking, "My brother got caught getting high, what an idiot." You know what I mean? I didn't think there would be this whole downward spiral, but I also don't think I fully understood the other issues he was having. I just thought my older brother was sometimes hard to get along with and had trouble making friends. So, I'm thinking, "Why is he doing this stuff?" I thought he was just doing it because he wanted to fit in so badly that he would do anything at that point. I didn't think he was going to become a full-blown drug addict until he became a full-blown drug addict.

Daniel

Poem

In Defining OK

I, being quite prolific, and even more eccentric . . .

I hate to be esoteric;

Let's talk in plain terms then, agreed?

Each day we meet people on the streets

We exchange a nod

But I still walk away in agony.

Generally

When someone asks you how your day is going,
    we always respond this way

Oh yes I'm fine just great everything is ok

But moan while you walk away and groan under
    the weight of a bronzed oppression.

So don't ask me if I'm ok.

Don't inquire about my day.

Because I'm liable to be quite honest

Yes sir well I feel like I'd rather be dead

What if we said how we really felt instead

Of ok . . .

But who has the time

To stop on a dime

To listen to a man's complaints

Because hello is a customary process amongst strangers

To embrace this would mean the danger

Of being five minutes late to work.

The love of man is dissipating

And yes I am insinuating

continued

That this whole pipe dream shall end in tragedy
And that's why people hate me.
But I never liked them much anyway
Anyway
I'm not ok.
I'm really not ok.

(date unknown)

CHAPTER 2

Motherhood

Long before I was an addict's mom, or a mom at all, I grew up in a working-class family in New York City—Queens, to be specific. After high school, I went off to college and majored in elementary education. I was planning on being a schoolteacher after college, and I think I would have loved that. But after I graduated, my mom told me about a competitive program she had heard about to learn computer science and programming. That was a well-paying, emerging field at the time, so I decided to try for it, and I got in. That led to a great job at a major holding company, where I quickly rose through the ranks and became head of mainframe training. I was still teaching, but rather than children, I was teaching other employees about computer science and the technological capabilities of the company. It was a great job, and I was really proud of my success, but other things started fighting for my attention.

In the late 1980s, I met my first husband in the office building where I worked. He worked in the bank on a lower floor, and he was handsome, charming, made a good living, and played guitar. We had issues from the beginning of our dating relationship—I don't even know how many times we broke up and got back together. He had a temper and I would get fed up with it, leave, and come back in a few weeks. We tried couples counseling, but it would always end in an unproductive argument. Yet part of me still loved him, and when he asked, I agreed to marry him. We had our first son, Peter, shortly after, and I decided to leave my job to be a full-time mother. When Peter was still a toddler, both my husband's parents and mine moved down to Florida, and when we went down to visit, we loved the area. So, we decided to follow them.

I have a lot of happy memories from those first few years in Florida. When Peter was still really little, I remember walking with him to the toy store. He was very smart from a very young age. We would walk around the toy store and pick up everything he liked and put it in the cart. Then we would sit down somewhere and go through the toys one by one, which turned into a game in itself. I would pick up each toy and say, "Okay, why would it be good to get this one?" and we would say the good things about each one until we decided which toy was the best one to buy. Then we had Daniel, then our daughter, Nicole. Having three children made everything a bit more complicated, but I loved having the ability to devote all my time to being a mom. Before we got a house, we lived in an apartment complex and met a lot of our neighbors. We had people over all the time, and I would take the kids to the beach almost every sunny weekend. On rainy days, the kids and I would make up games to play together inside. I would walk to the bookstore with Daniel, or watch movies and sing silly songs with Nicole, or we would all go to the city pool.

Unfortunately, having children didn't change the unhealthy dynamics of my marriage. My husband had traditional ideas of what our roles should be in the family. He went to work and made the money, and I was in charge of taking care of the children. It became more and more clear that we were two very different people, and we fought constantly. I tried to protect my children from the chaos, but everyone in the house was hurt and unhappy. My husband's anger would spill over onto the children, Peter and Daniel in particular, and I wasn't always there to protect them. In hindsight, I probably knew the marriage was a mistake before it even happened. I think I stayed with him as long as I did for a similar reason I became so devoted to helping Daniel later in life: I had a need to be needed, and I felt that he needed me.

I left my husband in my mind probably two years or more before we got divorced. In my experience, you often make decisions in your mind long before you finally work up the energy to execute them. There was a period of several months where we would break up, get back together, break up, get back together, on and on. He was raised to believe that it's important to keep a family together no matter what, so he strongly resisted the idea of divorce. But I think, after a while, he got just as exhausted of the back and forth as I was.

I was now a single mom, and that brought both happiness and stress. It was freeing and scary. After I moved out with the kids, I realized just how much we had all been walking on eggshells before. I now had space to breathe and the freedom to really focus on myself and my kids, but along with that freedom came heavy responsibilities. I went back to school to study physical therapy and tutored other students to help make ends meet until I got my degree. I needed to be more creative with our limited resources. Since I was Jewish and my ex-husband was not, we celebrated both Hanukkah and Christmas, but that year I didn't have money to buy presents for both holidays. So, I came up with a solution to keep some sense of normalcy that became a tradition. That year and every year after, instead of getting the kids gifts for Hanukkah, I made them coupons that could be exchanged for things like "Stay up all night, no questions asked." and "Get off grounding, no questions asked." They started looking forward to those just as much as their Christmas presents.

In hindsight, maybe that time was a missed opportunity to try to slow down and connect more with my kids in other ways. Maybe I should have talked to them more about the divorce and about their dad and how they were feeling about their lives—maybe that would have made some difference for their future. But that's easy to say now. Not so easy then, when balancing every little thing every day felt more like survival than really living. Just trying to find a place to live, trying to have enough money, trying to get through the day, trying to get the kids ready for the weekend, trying to be there for them. Being a single mother was all about survival.

About a year and a half after my divorce, a friend of mine met a guy at a party and thought he would be a good fit for me, so she set us up. He was young and hardworking. He had immigrated to the US from Greece as a teenager, put himself through school, and worked his way up to owning his own successful business. We connected right away, and he gave me the stability I needed. It really felt like a Cinderella story—he swept me off my feet. Rudy seemed to come into my life when I needed it most. The only wrinkle was that he wanted to have a child of his own. When we started dating, he didn't know that I hadn't planned on having any more kids after Nicole, so I'd had my tubes tied. We talked about it and decided I would have surgery to get it reversed. When I walked down the aisle, Peter, Nicole, and Daniel were there with me, and I was pregnant with our son Alexander.

Shortly before the wedding, I had just finished my prerequisite classes and been accepted into a master's program in physical therapy. But I was also about to have another baby. So, again, I decided to put my career on hold to be a full-time mother. As my kids got older and all of them were in school during the day, my lack of career started to weigh heavy on me. I was home alone all day until around 3 p.m., and I was getting restless. I still wanted to be free when my kids came home from school, but I wanted a chance to get out and meet people, and to learn things and problem-solve the way I had in my training job. I decided to try to organize a group of women to meet around lunchtime, when a lot of people would be available. That idea developed into a group called the Women's Business Mastermind Group. We organized lunchtime meetings with women from all different fields to talk about our successes and challenges in work and life. The women did presentations for the group and made networking connections for each other. I started doing local PR for the group to attract new members. It kept me active and connected, and it was rewarding to see all the women bonding and learning from each other.

Talking to all of those women made me want to get back into a career of my own, so I started taking classes at the local university in family therapy. I really liked working with groups of people and helping solve problems, so I thought counseling would be a good fit. For a while, my life was plenty busy with the kids, my lunchtime group, and taking classes in the hopes of starting a new career. In 2008, all of those plans and routines changed. In quick succession, I received my master's degree in family therapy and found out my son Daniel was addicted to cough medicine. Shortly after that, through late-night tears sitting at my computer at my kitchen table, I started a Facebook group called The Addict's Mom (TAM).

I was still meeting with the Mastermind group, but my participation and leadership was clearly slipping. During the meetings, I started having to step out to take calls from Daniel, or from his treatment center, or from the hospital saying he had just been admitted. Other times, I would show up at the meetings with puffy eyes revealing that I'd had another sleepless night, or had just stopped crying over a crisis earlier in the morning. I was open with them about what was happening—I never thought of my son's addiction as something I needed to hide. A couple of times, when Daniel seemed stable, I took him to the meetings to talk about his experiences. I thought it might help the other moms understand their children, and Daniel said he felt like he was doing some good at a time when his self-esteem was very low. The women in the group were compassionate and supportive, but they could also tell I was drifting farther and farther away from anything that wasn't Daniel and his addiction.

The moms in the group didn't have addicted children, and there were only so many supportive things they could say. Other mothers started finding my new Facebook group, and I spent more and more time on my computer asking for help and updating them about Daniel's condition. As TAM kept getting bigger and bigger, Daniel kept getting worse, and it just became obvious what direction my life was going. I didn't have much, other than tears, to add to a women's business group anymore. So, I let go of my responsibilities in the women's group, I set aside any ideas I had about going back to work, and I fell into my life as the addict's mom.

When TAM first started, it was difficult to convince people to join. The common thinking was that if a child is using drugs, their parents must be to blame. No one wanted to admit to a group of strangers that they had "failed" as a parent. When mothers did join, they would often join with a new profile under a different name. No one wanted to risk information about their child's addiction appearing on their personal Facebook page. Slowly, as everyone became more comfortable with each other, that started to change. Once mothers found TAM, it became their lifeline. It certainly became mine. In the beginning, we were just a group of women talking to each other online, but after a while it became clear that we needed to set some boundaries in the group. Some women would give unsolicited opinions and judge others. They would tell others what they should and shouldn't be doing without listening to the specifics of that person's needs and situation. TAM was supposed to be a haven from those feelings of judgment. I wanted it to be a place where moms could seek out advice if they wanted it, but where they knew they wouldn't be blamed for sharing their true feelings and actions. So, I set and started enforcing rules about this. No blaming other moms for their or their child's decisions. No offensive language or bullying of members. What's shared in TAM, stays in TAM.

As time went on, more and more mothers became willing to join the group under their real names. They became more willing to meet each other in person, even if it was just a brief meeting in a café or a grocery store parking lot. They became more willing to write to their state senators, telling their story, or even appear in their local newspapers. They knew that they had a group of people who really understood them to catch them if they fell and who wouldn't blame them for whatever was happening to their child, whether they were improving or not. We started calling each other sisters, because that's really how it felt. I wrote to local newspapers and radio stations and told them about us and what we were doing, and they listened and wanted to spread the word. People joined from all over Florida, and from other states too. But as The Addict's Mom was starting to thrive, my own family was falling apart. I was getting more support and advice than I could have possibly imagined, but none of it was saving my son.

■

Family

When I married Barbara, I knew her three kids were part of the equation, and I was okay with that. I didn't have any kids from my previous marriage and wanted to have a child of my own. I was thinking both in the short term and the long term. I really loved her. We would raise the kids together, then eventually they would grow up and follow their own paths and live their own lives. Then, Barbara and I would spend the rest of our lives together.

Even when everything is going well, having six people in one household is going to cause friction. Every person is different, and as a parent you have to worry about everything. Going to work to support everyone, buying things for them, cooking, cleaning, and interacting with everyone in a different way depending on their needs. Then you add in all the complications of having a blended family. Then Daniel is bothering the other kids and not respecting everyone's boundaries, and he's getting in trouble at school, and we start worrying about Peter's eating, and we need to take Nicole to dance practice, and Alex is just a baby so we have to make sure he's protected. All of those things add up quick.

Imagine that you're in that scenario and then you break a leg. When it happens, you have to walk on crutches or whatever and everyone feels bad for you. But then the effects from your broken leg get so bad that it's preventing everyone else from having dinner, or from going out, or from sleeping at night. All of a sudden, the broken leg is not just your problem. It's a huge problem for your family.

As a parent, you try to give a certain percentage of energy to yourself, a certain amount to your job, and a certain percentage to each person in your family. When one of those people living in your house has an addiction, that person now requires 80 or 90 percent of your energy. You're running on empty all of the time. Trying to do anything about it is almost like trying to jump-start a dead battery. As much as you try, the car never really cranks. It's an exercise in futility.

After Daniel's addiction got going, it was nonstop. We tried everything imaginable to get him help, but it just never stuck. He went from rehab to rehab to halfway house, and it was always the same story. When he was living with us, he would be high around Alex when Alex was only six, seven, or eight years old. I would find empty cough syrup bottles and pill wrappers in Alex's bathroom. Daniel rented a room in our friend's house and got kicked out after a month. He tried to live with his dad and only ended up staying about two weeks. He would come to our house high as a kite and jump me or yell at Barbara, and I had to call the cops on him several times. And then it got to the point where we had to unplug the phone because he would call at two, three, four in the morning. He then resorted to knocking on our door, when I had to get up to work the next day. I always lived with the fear of being stalked, because I never knew when he was coming.

I do believe that addiction is a disease. Once it starts, it's really hard to stop, and families can give their kids the tools to make it easier. But that's all they can do. Ultimately, it has to end in a choice. The addicted person has to realize that they're in a bad position, make a decision to use the tools to get out of it, and really commit to getting clean. Just like any big goal in life, being drug free is something you have to commit to and work really hard to achieve. I never saw any signs that Daniel was doing that.

When you have a situation where a person is doing drugs and nothing is working, when the person is causing all this harm to our family and my wife is coming apart at the seams, you reach a breaking point. He was difficult when he was sober, and a nightmare when he was on drugs. It caused a lot of conflict between Barbara and me because we had different views and goals. She wanted to save him at all costs, and I wanted the problems to go away. I didn't want that stress and unpredictability around my family. I didn't want it around my son. I didn't want it around me. So, it reached a point where the two of us couldn't really talk about it. When she couldn't talk about it with me, she went to The Addict's Mom.

The point is, this family went to hell and back because of addiction. I don't think anyone can really understand what it's like until they go through it themselves, but I wouldn't wish that on anyone.

Invisible

Talking about my childhood is tough for a couple of reasons. First, there are a lot of things I don't remember, and other things I would rather not remember. I've learned that in order to keep the positive trajectory of my life now, I have to know my boundaries and avoid living in the past. Second, my relationships with my family have improved a lot in the last several years, and I don't want to do anything to jeopardize that. All that being said, it's impossible to tell my story without acknowledging some of the dynamics and difficulties of my early life.

I'm the oldest of my siblings: three years older than Daniel, five years older than Nicole, and eleven older than Alex, so in some ways, it makes sense that our childhood memories would be different. I remember moving around a lot as a kid. I was born when my parents were still living in New York, though I was too young then to remember that. We moved down to Florida for a few years, moved to North Carolina briefly when my dad got a job there, then back to Florida. We moved again when my parents got divorced, then again when my mom got remarried. Finally, I decided to move in with my dad right before high school and stayed there until I moved away from home. There was a period in elementary and middle school when I moved to a new school every year. It was really hard to make friends because I was always going somewhere new, and my birthday was in August, during the summer, so I almost never had the traditional birthday parties with friends from school. It became part of my identity that I would joke about—I was the kid who never stayed at a school more than a year. It was easy to joke about, but it was really isolating for a kid.

My parents had a chaotic relationship and then divorced when I was seven or eight. Even at that age, I could tell they weren't good together, so I was happy about the divorce. I don't have any memories of them being affectionate with each other before they separated. I don't think my mom has any regrets about it now, but I know the divorce affected her. I have a vivid

memory from right after we moved into our little apartment with my mom—
I walked in on her in the kitchen sitting on the floor with her back against
the refrigerator just crying to someone on the phone.

Both before and after the divorce, my mom spent a lot of time taking
care of Daniel. When he was a baby, he cried all the time, and when he
entered preschool, he started having behavioral issues right away, and she
was constantly talking to teachers and taking him to see doctors. At home,
he always wanted attention, even if it was negative. A couple years later,
my mom married Rudy and had Alex, so there was another baby in the
house to take care of. I know Rudy tried his best, and I admire his
willingness to jump into a household with three kids, but the two of us
never really had a father-son relationship. Daniel, Nicole, and I went to
my dad's house every other weekend, but I don't have great memories of
that either. Almost any attention I got from my dad was negative. In a lot
of ways, I felt like an invisible child.

I think I was around five when I started noticeably gaining weight. I
didn't make the connections until much later, when I started dating my
current girlfriend, who is a dietitian, but it's clear now that I started using
food as a coping mechanism to deal with my emotions at a very young
age. My family tried various things to help me lose weight or eat healthier—
some things that seemed helpful to some degree and others that probably
did more harm than good. Either way, nothing really worked. I realize now
that them trying to change my eating was actually them trying to treat the
symptom without addressing the underlying issues. By late middle school,
I had gained a lot of weight, and neither the kids at school nor my dad at
home were particularly kind about it.

Though I didn't have many friends at school, I did make friends in my
neighborhoods and through my hobbies. My two best friends growing up
were brothers who lived right near my dad, and we liked to hang out at the
game store down the street and play *Magic: The Gathering*. When I was
thirteen and about to go to high school, my dad asked me to move in with
him and I agreed. I wasn't excited to live with my dad, but he was in a better

school district, he was closer to my friends and my hobby, I was exhausted by the chaos of my mom's house, and I was ready for a change.

After that, my parents provided money and the essentials I needed to live, but I did a lot on my own. I kept my grades up, at least for a while, and when I did start coping by using things stronger than food, I hid it well. My dad didn't ask much about my life, and I only saw my mom, Rudy, and my siblings occasionally once I moved out. No one really thought to talk to me about my feelings and, as a teenager, it wasn't like I was seeking them out for life advice. For a long time, I just went to school, played games with my friends, handled my own business, and hoped that I would get left alone.

Daniel

Poem

Me

I am a unique individual
I'm so happy to be me
Despite what others see
My different thinking sets me free

I love to stare into the sky
As blazing sunlight hits my eyes
I see the wind rustle the leaves
Upon the ancient and majestic trees

I love color, music bathes my ears in ecstasy
My whole body in euphoric sensation
I feel my worries evacuating
Leaving my mind clear
And it's these times I so easily breathe
I couldn't think of a need

When people say that I'm spaced out
I simply smile, shrug, and laugh to myself
They have no idea I have such wealth
I used to say I'll say it again
In the end
I'd like a small home with a view of the sea
A groovy chick sitting next to me
It's come to be all I need

(2009)

CHAPTER 3

Daniel's Childhood

Before Daniel tried DXM, he tried to abuse Tylenol. I found out later that he told another kid at school about the Tylenol, and the kid said, "Why are you doing that? Why don't you take DXM? Like cough syrup and Triple Cs—that will give you a great high." Once he found DXM, that was it for him. But it was clear that the DXM was only one part of the problem. He didn't just go to a party, decide to try something, and then get hooked. And he didn't break his leg and get a prescription for opioids. He was willing to try anything that crossed his path. He was looking for something to help him escape his life.

From the day he was born, Daniel cried and screamed most of the time. Whenever I put him down to sleep or nap, he would just cry until he eventually exhausted himself. Shortly after he started preschool, the teachers pulled me aside and told me that he wasn't getting along well with the other kids. His peers weren't inviting him to play with them, and he would touch their things without permission and interrupt class with off-topic questions. They told me they thought something was wrong with him and told me I should look into medication. At that time, I just didn't like the idea of putting a child that young on behavioral medication. After what I had gone through with my brother, I was very cautious about any kind of mood-altering medications, prescribed or not. So, I decided against it.

Daniel's favorite toy as a child was an action figure of Jafar from *Aladdin,* which he watched all the time. He lost that toy several times, and each time it seemed like the end of the world for him. He wouldn't stop crying and begging until I went out and bought another one. I probably bought him more than a dozen Jafars just to keep some peace in our already chaotic household. I remember taking him to counseling when he was twelve. During the session, the psychologist got so frustrated with Daniel he yelled at him to be quiet. He apologized profusely for losing his temper, but he also told me Daniel would probably end up in jail. Daniel ended up seeing dozens of therapists, counselors, and psychiatrists over the years of his childhood and later addiction, and he was given several different diagnoses. They all described at least some of his behavioral and emotional issues, but nothing really clicked for Daniel or me, and none of those diagnoses led to a clear solution.

He was bullied from a young age. There was a kid who rode the bus with Daniel and Nicole who would always kick Daniel when he got on the bus. Once, I found kids in our neighborhood grabbing sticks and branches from a tree and throwing them at him. I remember one time when I went to pick him up from the movie theater. I wasn't expecting to get out of the car, so I was wearing my pajamas. I pulled up and saw other kids punching and kicking him out in front of the theater. I jumped out, grabbed him away from the boys, and led him, crying, to the car.

Despite all of that, he usually kept a very positive attitude. When he came home from school, he would seem happy and almost never told me anything was wrong. But when he got older and started using, he began opening up to me about his life. He told me that in middle school, when he was disruptive in class or bothering another student, the teacher would use a punishment called "internal suspension." They would take him out of class and leave him in a room all by himself, and they used that punishment for Daniel frequently. To him, that confirmed that he wasn't normal and deserved to be excluded. He didn't intentionally cause trouble in school; it was more like he was overly nice. He would try to reach out and connect to people and sometimes just didn't know when to stop. I loved him so much that I couldn't understand why other people couldn't see how brilliant and kind he was.

At home, he looked up to his big brother with awe and tried to protect his little sister from anything that bothered her. If I grounded her, he would come to me afterward and try to make the case for why she didn't deserve it. In the mornings, he would run into my room and jump on me and his father, telling us it was time to get up and how much he loved us. He was always interested in learning, and reading in particular. He and I would make frequent trips to the bookstore to get him something new to read and notebooks for him to write in. It was clear that during the times when he felt truly valued and supported, he did much better. I remember his third-grade teacher really tried to get to know him and support him. That year, he got straight As and won a Student of the Year award.

In middle school, he started reading the Bible. He took a big interest in it and memorized a lot of it. He was really interested in Jesus's teachings and wanted to feel connected to something bigger than himself. But he also struggled with how much of it he truly believed. My family is Jewish, and Daniel's father isn't religious. We celebrated Hanukkah and Christmas, but never emphasized any religion with the kids. I didn't really understand what made Daniel so interested, but I was happy to encourage anything that helped him feel happy. One day I stopped at a church in our neighborhood and asked them if they had a youth group, and if Daniel could start attending. I was desperate to find him a place where he felt like he belonged. They said yes, and I started taking him there. At first, it worked. He was clearly happier and getting good grades in school again. But eventually, some of the kids there started making fun of him too, and his self-esteem deteriorated again.

Looking back, right before I found out he was using DXM, there was an increase in incidents. I pulled up to his high school to pick him up one day and saw a kid just push Daniel to the ground in front of everyone. I got called in to the school a couple weeks later because a kid had punched Daniel in the eye after Daniel talked back to him. Some kids first start using drugs at a party with friends, or even because they're prescribed. Daniel started because he wanted something—anything— to help him get out of his own head and escape what was happening in his life. Someone told him DXM could do that, and that was it.

One of my favorite memories of Daniel is a vivid picture that I have from Mother's Day when he was in middle school. I remember looking out the window in the morning and seeing him walking down the side-walk toward the house. He was holding a bouquet of flowers in front of him with both hands. He had woken up early and walked to the store by himself to buy them for me. He looked so happy and was looking down at the flowers, like he was trying to concentrate to make sure he didn't damage them. Mother's Day always meant a lot to him. Later on, when he was in jail or in a rehab facility, he still never forgot to do something special for me. The first Mother's Day I spent without him was when he was spending nine months in a juvenile detention facility. He made me a Mother's Day card and sent it in the mail. It was a poem that began and ended with the line "On this Mother's Day, the past does not exist." He meant this in a positive way—he was sorry for the pain he had caused me in the past, and he wanted to put the baggage of his past behind him, at least for a day. That was the first of many holidays when my family would not be together. On Thanksgiving and Christmas, there would be an empty chair at the table that represented the elephant in the room. Instead of a holiday signifying tradition and love and happiness, I had to just do my best to get through it.

When it became more and more clear that Daniel's self-esteem was badly damaged, I did everything I could to counter his sadness. I would tell him that he was important and make him say it back to me. When he was upset and telling me he wished he was normal, I would ask him, "Daniel, what are you?" and he would know to answer, "I'm important." I would emphasize, "Yes, I love you, and you're important to me, you're important to your friends and family, and you're important to the world." I tried to make sure he never forgot that.

Childhood

When I was very little, before I was old enough to really have friends of my own, Peter, Daniel, and I were pretty close. I was the youngest, and the only girl, but Peter and Daniel involved me in whatever they were doing. We would play in the pool, or watch *Dragon Ball Z,* or I would play video games with them. If one of them was playing a one-player game, I'd happily sit and watch. I don't think a lot of older brothers involve their little sisters like that, and it definitely had an influence on my interests and personality as I grew up. Especially when we went to our dad's house on weekends, we kind of just had each other.

I think that, being the only girl, my parents had different standards for me. I would get in trouble for little things like staying on the phone too long. Whenever Daniel saw me upset, he would go to my parents and defend me. He would tell them I didn't really do anything bad and try to convince them to let me off grounding or whatever. One of my favorite memories of him at that time was on one of my birthdays. I don't remember how old I was, but Daniel, Peter, and I were all big into collecting Pokémon cards. I woke up on the morning of my birthday and saw dozens and dozens of cards spread out all over my bedroom floor. Daniel had come in while I was still sleeping and given me all of his cards for my birthday. Those things were like gold back then, so it was about as generous as a brother could get.

That's not to say we didn't have issues. For the first several years of my life, Daniel and I shared a room. I've always been a really light sleeper, and I couldn't have any light on when I was going to bed. But Daniel was afraid of the dark, so he always wanted to have a night-light on. So, almost every night, we would argue about the night-light. He would turn it on, I would get up and turn it off, and he would turn it back on again. It was exhausting. When I finally got my own room, Daniel's lack of boundaries became the big issue. Rudy had to buy a lock for my door because Daniel would constantly barge in and bother me or touch my stuff.

It probably wasn't until middle school when I started to realize some of Daniel's actions went beyond typical big brother behaviors. We were in different grades, so I didn't see him a lot in school, but I did start to see how he interacted with other people. I noticed that some of the things that I just thought of as a little annoying came off very different when he was acting that way around other kids. The difference was, I'm his sister, and these people didn't know him like I did or owe anything to him; they were just his peers. I guess the best way to describe it would be that he had impulses that he couldn't control. For example, let's say there's a pen on the table in front of me. In my head I might think, "It would be really funny to throw this pen across the room," but I wouldn't do it because my mind would tell me that's not appropriate. Something that I would think about before doing, he would just do it. He just had impulses. He had bad boundaries, and he just couldn't control himself in the same way that other people could.

I know he got bullied for being different. I didn't see a lot of it, but in middle school, we rode the bus together and I know there was one kid who picked on him all the time. One day when we were boarding the bus to go home, the kid challenged Daniel to a fight. They both got off the bus and the other kid, who was much bigger than Daniel, just beat him up in front of everyone. When Daniel got back on the bus, he had his head down and was clearly really upset and looked totally defeated. Everyone was laughing at him. It was a terrible moment for me, watching that and knowing I couldn't do anything about it. And I know it affected him for a long time too. He wrote about that kid in his journals years later.

Peter also got picked on growing up. Before and shortly after I was born, my parents moved around a lot. I was too young to remember or really be affected by it, but Peter changed schools several times, and that made it hard for him to make friends. Since he was so much older, I was never in the same school as him, so I never saw him being bullied, but I saw him when he came home and knew it was happening. I never had those kinds of problems, which sort of made me feel guilty. Peter eventually made some good friends in my dad's neighborhood, but Daniel was often alone growing up. I think it made Daniel feel worse to see me succeeding at school and having relationships that he wanted and didn't have.

I don't remember the day when Peter moved in with my dad. I was about eight years old. I was still going to my dad's house every other weekend at that point, so I still saw him a lot. I think between all the things going on when I was growing up, like everything happening with my brothers, and Alexander being just a baby, I really focused a lot on myself and getting myself through. I knew my parents had plenty of other things to deal with, so I never asked for help with homework and I never asked for help with the little conflicts I had with friends. I kind of just did what I needed to do.

As we got older, Peter got made fun of and Daniel got made fun of; then we found out they were both using drugs. In comparison, my issues seemed like normal teenage girl issues. It was boys and friends and stupid things that I knew I could take care of myself, so I just did.

Peter

Damage

By the time I moved in with my dad and started high school, I was clearly on a downward trajectory. I still had a few solid friends that I hung out with outside of school, but I didn't know anyone at my new high school. I was still gaining weight and getting bullied for that, and I didn't have a great home life. When I was around fifteen or sixteen, I was in such a negative mental space that I was willing to do pretty much anything that might help get me out of it. People at school were getting high, and joining them was a way to both make friends and temporarily feel good. I was willing to try just about anything.

I never really liked alcohol, but I started using pot and Triple Cs and it just accelerated from there. By late high school, I had tried cocaine, Xanax, and eventually painkillers. Once I stopped caring about myself completely, it was very easy to say, "Oh, this is available, let's do it. If it makes me feel better, I want it." As a bonus, using drugs was making me lose weight, and some people even started complimenting me on it, not knowing the reasons why it was happening. I liked the feeling of opioids much more than I liked uppers, so that's eventually what I stuck with. It was either my senior year of high school or shortly after that I injected heroin for the first time. I had some people over to my dad's house when he was out of town, and I let one of my best friends shoot me up, since I had never used a needle before. I knew at the time that it was a significant moment. I remember thinking, "My uncle was a heroin addict. If I do it, I'm going to get addicted." But at that point, I just didn't care. I had no self-esteem, so the threat of doing damage to myself meant nothing to me. I wanted to feel good, and I had already crossed so many lines. Anything can become normal if you do it long enough.

Throughout all of this, I managed to stay in school and graduate on time, but I had long since stopped caring about anything having to do with school. I had always been naturally smart, and they placed me in easy classes since I rarely completed my assignments, so I managed to just coast by without putting much effort into it. There were a few close calls. One morning a security guard caught me sleeping in my car in the school parking lot when I was supposed to be in class. I said I just fell asleep on accident and he was going to let me go to class, but he found a pack of cigarettes in my pocket. I was underage, so he took me to the office. They called my dad and printed out my list of absences, which was like three pages long. My dad was furious and was starting to realize something was happening with me, but he dropped the issue eventually.

Another time, my seventh-period teacher called my house because I had missed so many of her classes. My dad was home, but I lucked out and answered the phone before him. I basically told her, "Look, I know you don't understand this, but you're going to get me killed if you talk to my dad. I promise I'll be in class tomorrow." She let it go, and I went to her class every day after that. In general, my parents were just totally unaware of what was going on. Maybe since I had done well in middle school, they just assumed I would be fine in high school. I also like to think I did a good job of hiding everything.

After graduating high school, I got accepted to a university and went for a semester and a half. I just did my usual routine of getting high every day and skipping classes and they eventually put me on academic probation. I called my dad and said, "I hate it here; I want to come back," and he helped me move back into his house. I enrolled in a different college closer to home where I could take classes at a slower pace. I still didn't do great, but I managed to get my associate's degree. While taking classes, I got a part-time job and moved in to a house with some friends of mine. At that point, I was in really rough shape, and everyone who saw me regularly knew what was going on. The guy who owned the house actually wanted to say something to my parents, but another friend of mine convinced him not to. Eventually though, I couldn't keep up on rent and he kicked me out. I went to my mom's house and asked to stay there for a bit until I found another place. That's when she and Rudy finally began to suspect something was wrong. Rudy pulled up my sleeve and noticed a big abscess on my hand, and I made up some excuse. I wasn't sure if he was buying it, but getting caught was pretty much the worst thing I could imagine at that point, so I had to try. A little bit later I asked my mom for money, and she gave me a CD she wanted to return at Walmart. She said if I did that for her I could keep the $12 or whatever. I remember I was in the car and had just pulled out of the driveway when I saw Rudy speeding up to the house. He looked angry and motioned for me to pull over and get out, and then I knew what was going on.

Daniel

Poem

Mother's Day

On this Mother's Day

The past does not exist

Free from pain upon a mountain in eternal bliss

A selfless love, a beautiful love, only a mother has

Everything else may fade; a mother's love shall never pass

You have been there all my life to comfort me, and dry my tears

Schools, hospitals, psychiatrists, where have we not been
together throughout the years

And I'm so glad I shared such happy times with you

Remember taking me to lunch, just you and me, whenever
I felt blue

I don't know why my path has gone so astray

But please don't suffer in any way

Because one day

All the pain of Earth will fall away

And nothing will destroy our joy

So this Mother's Day the past does not exist

Free from pain upon a mountain in eternal bliss

(2010)

CHAPTER 4

Blue Mommy and Blue Peter

Once it really sunk in that Daniel was addicted to drugs, I couldn't imagine feeling anything worse. Then, about six months later, the unimaginable happened. After noticing some strange behavior from my oldest son, Peter, Rudy went over to the house where he had been staying. There, he discovered the horrible truth that we didn't have just one addicted son—we had two. I was at our condo about an hour away to try to get a break from everything happening with Daniel. Rudy called me there and told me what Peter's roommate had told him: Peter was using heroin and had a serious problem. As hard as it was with Daniel, this was a kind of pain I hadn't experienced yet. Since he was a baby, Daniel made it very clear that he needed my attention, and I had been doting on him just as long. At least I was confident that Daniel knew I loved him and would be there for him no matter what. In contrast, the discovery that Peter may have needed me just as much was accompanied by a lot of guilt and regret.

Peter was my first baby. He was beautiful and happy, and I was thrilled to be his mother. When he first started riding the bus to school, I would watch him walk to the bus stop every morning. He would always walk backward for a while so he could look back at me and wave goodbye. When he turned around to get on the bus, he would put his hand behind his back and keep waving. Since he started school, teachers always told me he was gifted. He got As on nearly everything. Also, unlike Daniel, even when Peter was having a rough time at school or home, he always had a few close friends to hang out with. He spent a lot of time at his friends' houses as he got older, and I knew he was close with their families. He also had social hobbies—he played video games with his friends and hung out at the local card shop. Although I would like to think I tried to be there for all of my children, I also know that from the beginning I felt that Daniel needed my help the most.

Yet I know there were many signs that Peter stopped being that happy baby pretty quickly. Being my oldest child, he was the most aware of the bad relationship between his father and me. We moved houses several times when he was young, so he changed schools and neighborhoods during his most formative years. When he was four years old, Peter painted me a picture and called it "Blue Mommy and Blue Peter." It shows him and me standing next to each other painted in different shades of blue. When he gave it to me, I was just thrilled that he had made something especially for me. I had it framed, and it's still hanging in my house today. Maybe even then he was trying to tell me something with those cool, blue tones. When he got older, maybe I just couldn't admit to myself he hadn't been my happy little boy for quite a while.

When Peter finished junior high, when he was about thirteen and his father and I had been separated for a few years, Peter decided to move out and go live with his father. I knew in my gut that this was a bad idea, and I told him so. I had seen his father's anger firsthand and didn't want my son living there. I was his legal guardian so I could have stopped him, but I didn't. Looking back, I was exhausted. Alex was still a toddler, Nicole was starting to need me to bring her back and forth from activities, and Daniel needed constant attention. Peter wasn't the type to ask for attention when he needed it. He tended to handle things on his own, and I was busy, so I let him. I know now that none of that is an excuse, but I do think it is the reason that I didn't try harder to resist.

I still saw Peter throughout his high school years, but not nearly as often. He didn't live with me, and we weren't as close. I became aware that he wasn't doing very well in high school—his grades were slipping, and that should have told me something was really wrong. But he still graduated on time and went off to college. Then he came back home from school, saying he didn't like it. Another bright red flag I didn't see, or chose not to. At that time, Daniel was worsening by the day. I kept myself in constant triage mode. I needed to get Alex to the sitter, get Nicole to dance practice, and then turn all my attention to Daniel, who seemed to be dying in front of me. I never stopped to think that Peter may have needed me just as much, just a little bit farther out of my sight. When Rudy called me that day in 2008, Peter was nineteen and I had never even seen him take a drink. I didn't even know he had tried pot. I had no idea what was going on with him.

By then, at least from all my research for Daniel, I knew what I was supposed to do. Peter had a drug problem, so he had to go to treatment. I told him that, and he agreed. When he got out, he got a place to live away from his father, got a job, started exercising, and seemed to be doing really well. But now I was aware of my failings. I knew he wasn't okay, and I needed to pay attention. A little over a year after he got out of treatment, I noticed he was starting to isolate himself again. I could tell something wasn't right, so I told him, "Peter, if something is wrong, you can tell me. I promise I won't judge you. You can tell me." A couple of weeks later, he stopped by one night when I had some friends over for dinner. He asked me to come outside because he had something to tell me. We sat in the car, and he told me he was using again. This time, I was ready for it. I tried to stay calm and just said, "Okay. Tomorrow you need to go back to treatment. You can do this again."

After that second stay in treatment, he really turned his life around. He worked incredibly hard, going back to school, getting a good job, and staying healthy. He has been in recovery since 2010, and I couldn't be more proud of him. Yet I'm not going to say the years since then have been easy for our relationship. When I was the most enmeshed with Daniel's life, Peter decided he needed to distance himself from it. He and Daniel had not been close for a while at that point, and Peter felt that being around Daniel's destructive behaviors was threatening his own recovery. Peter's recovery allowed me to be more hopeful for Daniel's future, but it was devastating to me that two brothers with such similar experiences couldn't have a healthy relationship. I made an effort to stay more connected to my oldest son, but when Daniel needed me most, I often neglected everything else.

The first time Peter went to treatment, I remember having an emotional breakdown in a session with his counselor. I was going on and on about how I didn't know if I could handle this, how I didn't have the money to pay for his treatment, how angry I was at my ex-husband. The counselor stopped me and said, "This isn't about you. It's about your son."

Out of all of the horrible lessons I've had to learn over the last ten years, that's probably the hardest. As a mother, it is easy to think of your children as an extension of yourself. When something goes wrong with them, it's easy to make it all about you. With Peter, I started by not being involved enough, which I think made it even more difficult to try to backtrack and find a healthy balance. But no matter what is happening in my life on any given day, I can now remember that I have one incredible son who has created a happy, healthy life for himself. I still treasure that painting Peter made for me as a little boy, but his recovery is the best gift he could have ever given me.

■

Peter

Treatment

By the time Rudy caught me, I had been living my self-destructive lifestyle for years and just didn't have any fight left in me. I didn't want to go to rehab, but I was also running out of resources, and I was gaunt, pale, and exhausted. After the blowup with Rudy, I fell asleep. I remember my mom coming in to tell me I was going to treatment in the morning, and I resigned myself to it. I just thought, "All right, I guess this is what happens when you're a drug addict."

First, I went to detox. I hadn't had any opioids in more than a day at that point, so I was getting pretty sick. Dilated pupils, cold and hot shakes, joint aches, and all that. I remember the nurse there being really sympathetic because she knew how bad it was to go through opioid withdrawal. She was like, "You poor guy," and gave me some medication to help me through it. I think I was there five days, and then they sent me to a treatment center.

At the treatment center, we had regular group therapy every day, I was in a trauma group once a week, and they took us to Narcotics Anonymous (NA) meetings. But a lot of rehab for me was just learning how to be an adult. They put me in a room with three other guys, and the two older guys taught me a lot. One of them taught me how to shave and do laundry. The other guy taught me how to shop and cook what I bought. I was nineteen, and I didn't know any of that stuff. My dad wasn't the kind of guy to sit us down and teach us to shave or whatever. Eventually they actually told my roommate to stop spending so much time teaching me to cook because they thought we would develop some kind of codependent relationship where I was relying on him.

My other, younger roommate and I also became really good friends— I actually still keep in touch with him. We were allowed to go to either the gym or the beach three or four times a week; we decided to go to the gym every time, and we stayed as long as we could. We didn't really know how to lift weights or use all the machines, but we figured it out. I started to lose weight and feel like I could actually start to control my life. I started to feel like I wasn't in a completely hopeless situation anymore, which was a huge change for me.

Being there got me away from my old life and patterns, got me away from my family, and exposed me to a bunch of people who had gone through similar experiences. I didn't identify with everyone there, but I did identify with their predicaments and their feelings. Everyone had their own terrible story to tell, and that helped normalize my experience. I think I just had to see that it wasn't totally abnormal for someone to be in the situation that I was in, given the circumstances that I had dealt with. I always felt like I should have been able to overcome it; I should have been able to deal with all the things that I dealt with and still have been skinny, and on the honor roll, and excelling at sports or whatever people do when they're successful. I thought because I hadn't achieved those outcomes that meant I was worthless. But being at the treatment center caused me to realize that for someone to go through the circumstances that I've gone through and even just be alive and doing okay is a monumental achievement. I started to see that other people also couldn't cope with the terrible experiences that they'd been through, and they needed help too.

By seeing that I wasn't the only one who was in this type of circumstance, seeing that other people had gotten through it by going to meetings, seeing people who were successful, and seeing people give their time back and sharing messages of positivity gave me a lot of hope too. People have been through my circumstance or worse, and they came out through the other side and have done okay. That gave me the confidence that, hey, maybe I can do it too. That was something that I had to see to really understand, I think.

Letter to Daniel

Dear Daniel,

I hope my letter finds you well and in good spirits. A lot has happened since I last saw you. Your brother Peter is in rehab once again, and this time I pray he will remain sober and is well on his way to recovery. He asked me about you and said he could not imagine how you have managed to go through so much and remain so strong. Daniel, once again this is another example of living in the world of addiction. Nobody is ever happy or productive on drugs. I can't imagine going through much more of this.

You are very special, and I want you to know that I believe in you. You must think positive thoughts and balance your life. You must say no to all drugs. I have always felt that you were very hard on yourself and that is what got you into trouble. You must love yourself and forgive yourself as you love and forgive others. I want you to remember that you are eighteen years old already and that you are an adult. While you need the love and respect of your family, you have to start looking at a future where you are self-reliant. You are smart and ambitious and dedicated to changing for the better. You have everything it takes to succeed if you remain drug free.

If you are wondering how Peter got into rehab, it was really very simple. He came over and told me, "Mom, I have something to tell you." I already knew what that was, and he said he needed help. I was very proud of him for asking me for help. Although I must admit I am running out of resources to help everyone. I pray that you and Peter start looking at your lives and decide to make better choices in the future. You must have a college education, and you must have a career. I need both of you to focus on creating a life for yourself that is meaningful.

Your sister Nicole is doing well, and so is your brother Alex. They both send their love, and Rudy says hello.

Love you,
Mom

(March 4, 2010)

Daniel

Letter to Mom

Dear Mom,

I feel guilty about our last phone call. At the time I couldn't really absorb the seriousness of what you told me. I'm so sorry to hear Peter relapsed. I know you must be really upset on top of the added stress. Dad and grandpa visited me this week, and I'm convinced I should at least get my associate's degree, so I talked with one of my teachers and we developed a plan. If I put my mind to it, I'm positive I can complete at least one course.

I know I'm an adult now and I want to help carry the finances, so I want to work as soon as I can. Then I can pay a portion of my rent and groceries, so try to find some work for me before I leave.

Mom, I am constantly thinking about my future. Every Sunday I work on a plan.

Freedom is still my number one priority so you know I'm bettering myself. I started reading *The Secret for Teens* and one thing I'm finally internalizing is living in the moment, not living for tomorrow. Living in the moment means I'm doing one thing at a time and making the most of each moment of the day.

Also, I've learned to give myself a break, and I congratulate myself on my little victories. Another great lesson, one of the most important, is I've learned to look on the bright side. Mom, you are so strong but you worry too much for your own health's sake. Don't live for your children. Support us, love us, but you have to realize that we are adults now and we will live our own lives.

Spiritually I'm doing well, I try and pray once a day. When I pray I feel serenity and sometimes when I'm super stressed I say the serenity prayer and I ask God to help me accept what I cannot change.

I think I am growing into an extremely intelligent, caring, and well-rounded person. It's funny, I think I've finally mastered this whole scheduling thing, because in the last two months I've made about a thousand schedules. I barely gave myself time to breathe! Now I value discipline and I also value leisure, and I'm learning to relax and not feel guilty. I'm working out but I'm not dieting because we don't get too much food in here and I get hungry.

Love you,
Daniel

(March 2010)

Nicole

Daniel and Peter

I don't remember my mom ever sitting us down to have a conventional talk about drugs and alcohol. But she was always very honest with us about the history of addiction and mental health issues in our family. Besides my uncle, there was a history of excessive drinking and depression on both sides of my family. She told us that family history meant that we may be predisposed to have problems with those things. That became much more apparent when it started affecting us directly.

After I first found out about Daniel's DXM use, he starting going downhill pretty quickly. He went to treatment, came back, relapsed, went to a different rehab, got kicked out of school, started stealing and getting arrested. . . . It was a nonstop cycle.

Peter was very different. I didn't have any idea he was using until my parents found out. He had been living at my dad's and then living with his friends, so I didn't have much regular contact with him at that point. He's also five years older than me, so we didn't have a whole lot in common to keep in touch about. It was very shocking to hear he was using heroin. I had to look up information on DXM when I found out Daniel was using it, but I didn't have to look up heroin. Even at that age, I was very aware of how dangerous it was. It was pretty much the worst possible thing he could be doing. And for me, it came out of nowhere. Luckily, his situation didn't become the cycle that Daniel's did. He went into treatment right after we found out and really turned his life around after that.

I tried to take care of myself and keep my life on track, but I also wanted to help Daniel and my mom however I could. I started going with her to visit Daniel in rehabs and jails and hospitals. The worst place I remember was probably Dade Juvenile Residential Facility (also known as DJRF), where he stayed the longest. From the first time I went there, a bunch of the other juveniles would catcall me every time. Whenever I'd walk up, I'd hear them yell my name. When we sat down, Daniel would tell me the gross things they were saying about me behind my back. Even if it was a really hot day, I would wear a sweater or a hoodie, hoping that if I didn't show any skin they wouldn't say anything. I really didn't like thinking that my brother was living in there with those guys.

When I got older and my mom or Daniel would call asking me to go somewhere, I would try to maintain some boundaries and gauge the severity of the situation. If it was a call saying Daniel had relapsed for the hundredth time and my mom wanted to go buy him a whole new wardrobe, I didn't feel like I had to take part in that. From the beginning, I thought the amount of stuff she would buy him again and again was excessive. But if it was something that I felt my mom really shouldn't have to do by herself, I would be there. I didn't want to go, but my mom didn't force me either. It became the lifestyle. It became my reality that if I want to see my brother, I'm gonna see him in rehab. Or jail. Or the hospital. It was either see him like that or don't see him. And often, it was more for my mom than for Daniel. I saw what she was going through, and I saw how much it was killing her. If it was between me being burdened and her having to do it by herself, I chose the former.

Different

By the time Daniel's addiction started, Peter had been living with his father for a while. Barbara and I didn't have any idea that Peter had that kind of problem. He asked us for money sometimes when he saw us, but what teenager doesn't? He seemed to be handling things pretty well on his own. Around the time we found out about Daniel, Peter was renting a room at his friend's house only about half a mile away from us. About six months after everything started with Daniel, Peter came over and told us he was moving out of his place and needed to stay with us for a bit until he could move in somewhere else. To me, the situation just didn't sound right. He was living with friends his same age who he liked, as far as I knew, so why would he want to move out all of a sudden? I ended up going over to their house and talking to the friend who he was renting from. I just said, "Hey, I heard Peter is moving out. I guess we need to make arrangements to pick up his stuff, but why is he moving out?" He goes, "Well, I asked him to move out. You know he's a heroin addict, don't you?" I told him no, I did not, and he took me to Peter's room. He showed me a bunch of needles and spoons and paraphernalia that were in there. I couldn't believe it. Nothing indicated to me that he was doing this. I took photos of all the stuff on my phone and drove home to confront him. He was pulling out of the driveway when I got there, so I motioned for him to go back. I showed him the photos and yelled at him, "What's going on here? Are you kidding me?" I just couldn't believe it. We had one addicted kid and now another on top of that. It was unreal.

In the end, though, I really have to give Peter credit. He was dealt a bad hand and took care of his issues much different than Daniel. He went to rehab, relapsed after a year and a half or whatever, went back a second time, and then he was done. He worked really hard and made a lot of improvements in his life. And even while he was using, he was still functioning, you know? Now, he's doing really well.

Barbara

Not a Miracle

TAM Facebook post

I was having coffee with my oldest son. We spoke about old times, new times, and life in general. At one point we were discussing our family members, which led us to touch on my addicted son Daniel.

I looked at my older son and then blurted out, "Peter it would take a miracle, God himself would have to come down from heaven and step in, in order to save your brother!" He looked at me with this crazy smile on his face and said "Mom, and what makes you think you are that miracle?"

Much love to all addicts' moms and their families.

Barbara

(February 26, 2014)

CHAPTER 5

Daniel's Addiction

Daniel's addiction lasted for eight long years and, to be honest, a lot of that time just feels like a nightmarish blur. It feels like an endless cycle of treatment, relapse, hospital, jail, mental health facility, back out on the street. . . . Rudy kept a time line of the major events for the first few years so we would have a record to show judges and lawyers to prove that he needed special care. Eventually, we stopped keeping track. After that, his addiction story is documented in his arrest record, in my posts on TAM, in his own journals, and in my painful, fragmented memories.

Daniel came home from his first stay in treatment feeling worse, not better. Regardless, there wasn't much we could think to do except try again. I had more hope about the second center because it specialized in youth with co-occurring addiction and mental health issues, which is what my son needed. And every interaction I had with the staff and location indicated that it was more reputable than the first and they were more interested in truly getting their patients well. After he arrived and completed an evaluation, they wanted to start him on psychiatric medications. Since he was still a minor, I had to give permission. I was reluctant, still hanging on to my fears that many medications could be dangerous to a child with a family history of substance abuse, but I knew now that this was serious, and the clinicians there seemed to know what they were doing. So, I gave my consent. Daniel got on the phone and screamed at me, cursing me out, which he had never done before in his life. I was so shocked and angry, I yelled back, "You're doing this, Daniel!

Don't call me again until you're done for good!" and hung up. Looking back, he surely picked up on my reluctance to put him on medications as a kid. After hearing me reject medications so many times, it made sense that he was scared of them. He completed the full month stay at the center but relapsed a few days after coming home.

In the next several months, the vicious cycle of Daniel's relapses and issues at school and home really started developing. Shortly after he turned seventeen, Daniel asked to be emancipated. He said Rudy and I were too controlling, and he wanted to live his own life as an adult. In reality, he meant that he wanted to get high in peace and didn't want us looking over his shoulder anymore. To Rudy, this seemed like a mutually beneficial arrangement—it meant that Daniel would no longer be bringing so much trouble home to us and would no longer be getting high in the house around Alex. Daniel was so close to being a legal adult already, as scary as that prospect seemed, and I knew Rudy was reaching the end of his rope. So I told Daniel I would sign the paperwork and pay for an apartment for him to help him get on his feet, but only if he graduated high school.

At that point, he had already been kicked out of two high schools and was on thin ice with a third. He got kicked out of the first after bringing alcohol to class, intending to sell it to buy more cough medicine. He started at another school and then overdosed in the middle of the day and had to be taken out by ambulance. The administration and I agreed that it would be best if he didn't come back after that. The whole school was talking about it, and I knew the other kids would never forget it. He was at his third high school when he asked to be emancipated. He only had about six weeks left of classes, so the vice principal told him he could finish the work at home and should be well prepared to take the GED test. He really encouraged Daniel and gave me a little bit of hope. He said that he had also gotten a GED rather than a high school diploma, and that a lot of employers really don't differentiate between them. I was grateful for his encouragement. Daniel listened to him and agreed to take the test. He passed, so I followed through on my side of the agreement, and he was emancipated a few months before his eighteenth birthday.

In the summer of 2009, Daniel was high and struggled to get away from a police officer who approached him, so he got arrested for the first time. The judge was going to let him go with a warning, but I begged her not to. It seems unimaginable to beg a judge to sentence your child, but I was so scared of Daniel overdosing again and dying, and none of the treatment seemed to be working. I thought, maybe if the judge sent him to some kind of long-term program, he could get completely off the DXM and that would finally make a difference. I wrote the judge a letter explaining the danger of the drugs my son was taking and included all of his psychiatric and hospital records. She agreed to send him somewhere, but since Daniel had been emancipated, he would have to consent. I told Daniel that if he refused to go to the long-term program, the judge would try him as an adult, and he would get a longer sentence in an adult jail. She didn't actually have any plans to do this, but he believed me and was afraid of being tried as an adult, so he consented. The judge sentenced him to nine months in the DJRF. The program served youth through the age of nineteen, so he could stay there for the full term. Looking back, this is another point where I can't help but wonder if I made a mistake. His time in DJRF was the longest he ever stayed sober, and his letters from that time show that it encouraged him to reflect on himself and his choices for the future. Overall, the staff were really good to him and, I admit, it was a relief to know exactly where I could find him for months at a time. Yet by pressing the issue with the judge, I sped up his entry into the criminal justice system, which would end up being a long and terrible relationship for both of us.

As the issues I and other mothers were facing with our children evolved, so did The Addict's Mom community. When it had become clear that Daniel and I would continue to be involved with the criminal justice system, I started the first offshoot group of TAM, for mothers with incarcerated children. When we started having more and more members joining who were raising their grandchildren due to their child's addiction, we created a group specifically for them. We created groups for dads and siblings, since they also needed support specific to their needs. It became more and more clear that everyone dealing with addiction in their family had a lot in common, and they also had a lot of specific needs that only people like them could truly understand. There is nothing more empowering than knowing there is a group of people waiting for you who are going through the same issues.

I also started reaching out to more and more experts and media outlets in my community and elsewhere. My attitude has always been, if there's someone I want to meet or someone I thought could help the moms of TAM, I would just reach out and ask for their help. That's something my dad taught me when I was little. He would say, "Asking for help is the most effective thing to do." When people heard about what we were going through as mothers with addicted children, they almost always wanted to do something to help. So, TAM started getting more media exposure and offers of scholarships from treatment centers, and I and other moms started being asked to speak at community events.

Daniel had a lot of privilege and advantages from the beginning of his addiction. Rudy had money he was willing to put toward treatment, at least at first, and the resources and knowledge I gained through TAM opened a lot of doors for both of us. I knew countless moms in TAM who could not afford to send their child to treatment without getting a scholarship. For them, being able to put their child in treatment once was huge, and there was so much riding on it. Meanwhile, Daniel cycled through several different centers and racked up medical bills without really showing any signs of change. Because of those privileges, there were some people we encountered who looked down on us. One time a prosecutor even remarked that she thought Daniel was getting special treatment he didn't deserve because of my connections. I was appalled. Was I actually hurting him more than I was helping him by giving him every option I could come up with? But what mother wouldn't do everything possible to get her child well if she had the chance?

At times, Daniel acknowledged his privileges and told me how grateful he was for everything we were doing to help him. He would promise that, this time, things would be different. He would take full advantage of this fourth, or seventh, or tenth chance and really stay sober and start an independent life. Then, he would take another turn for the worse and complain that Rudy and I were too harsh, that he hated being in those facilities, that I could never really understand his relationship with DXM, and that he was doing just fine without us. It was an exhausting transformation to witness over and over again. One thing I will say, however, is that he always seemed to recognize the importance of helping those less fortunate. Whenever I was angry with someone else, he would stress to me the importance of forgiving others and giving back, quoting Bible passages. He was also proud of what I had done with TAM and was happy I had that support system. He gave me his writings to share on TAM as a way of trying to help other parents understand what their children were experiencing. He understood and demonstrated the importance of sharing without shame.

Daniel

Poem

Dark Side of the Moon

From mothers who would give their life to see you make it

Saying things like "your age is the hardest age, you've got to believe that"

And from fathers who say "promise me you won't do it again"

Brothers who don't believe you can do it,

And sisters who weren't surprised to see you go

To yourself, who finds that death might just be the end to an endless amount of problems in your life

To the church, who wonders how the boy teaching sermons turned to drugs to solve his problems

To friends who don't call you day after day

And friends without friends who count on someone who can't even count on themselves

To the school crowds I linger around without truly being a part of

To a girlfriend who doesn't know me and will probably not take me back

To books that will go unread

To poetry that is in the trash,

To poetry that can never be replicated again

To misery that doesn't love company

To God that wishes I were with him

To the Devil offering his advice

To workouts that provide momentary hope,

And success that I fear

To neighbors who forget you and say
"Is that a cigarette in your hand?"
And to all these, they don't know me,
And even I don't know myself and maybe never will.

(circa 2010)

Letter to Daniel

Dear Daniel,

I asked one of the girls that I work with if she could switch days with me so I could get Sunday off so I could come up to see you, but unfortunately she couldn't switch with me. I will make sure that I get a Sunday off soon. I really miss you. There have been numerous occasions where stuff has happened that I only want to talk to you about and I can't. I want you to promise me that when you get out you're really going to turn over a new leaf and not get in trouble again because seriously I don't want to see you gone somewhere where you're not happy for a long time again. If you can't do it for yourself, do it for me. It'd be nice to have my brother around like old times. Mom keeps saying when you get out we're gonna go away for a couple of days. I'm really looking forward to it. I'm almost on summer break, which means I only have one more year home and then I go off to college. I think that will be good for me. As much as I love our whole family, we have all been through so much that I need to get away. But you will definitely be able to come up and stay with me. I hope you're still doing well at DJRF. Last time I spoke with you, you seemed like you were handling the situation really well. I'm really proud of how strong you are being. I would never be able to put up with everything you are putting up with there. It's funny because you think I am an inspiration to you but I think the exact opposite. You have been through so much, and I have never seen someone be able to deal with so much so amazingly. Now it's time for you to turn your life around, and I know you can do it. You're going to learn there is so much more to life than doing wrong things that hurt your body. I promise in time it will get easier. You are stronger than you ever think you are, and you have my support whenever you need me. Not too much longer, hang in there! Love you.

Love,
Nicole

(2010)

Daniel

Journal Entry

Serenity Scene

Clear your mind and imagine the creative spirits surrounding you, adorning you with new insight.

Even when constant voices fill the air, a quiet place awaits. A bench and a boy looking into clear blue skies at clouds that say, with overwhelming voices, "Even though the whole world is living to die, you must not. No worries."

Even now I hear it, so I close my eyes and imagine the time in my life when the rules were not black and white, not yielding terrible consequences. And oppression, if even for a moment, took its steel hand from blocking the sun.

I can't and may never see such a sun again, but I need to remember that I can always imagine better times.

(2010)

Barbara

The Addict's Brother

TAM Facebook post

My little son Alex, 11, came home today and decided to paint.
He painted pictures of him and his brother Daniel and titled them
"The Addict's Brother." Now he tells me he is writing a book
called "The Addict's Brother." He has only seen his brother Daniel
a few times this year and I know it hurts him. This woke me up
even more to how much he needs me, and how much pain he is in.
Regret is a useless emotion, but I wish I hadn't obsessed so much
over my addicted sons. I had two other children who needed me too!
I still believe it is never too late to live in the solution. Each day is an
opportunity to spend time with Alex and be a mom who is present.

(September 22, 2011)

Daniel's Emancipation

Daniel's story is very different from Peter's. It wasn't long after we found out about Peter that I reached a breaking point with Daniel in our house. Daniel also was getting tired of having to follow our rules, so when he turned seventeen, he asked to be emancipated. The day before he was supposed to move out, I asked him to please try to clean his room and get his stuff out of the bathroom before he left. With all the kids, I've always been big on them respecting the rules and taking responsibility for their parts of the house.

I was at a banquet for Barbara when Nicole called us and said Daniel was acting strange. I didn't want to interrupt Barbara's night, so I went home to check on them. When I get there, I see this huge mess. Daniel's room and the bathroom were a disaster area! Seeing all that mess, and the disrespect it represented, just triggered a huge response in me. All of the anger at putting our family through everything he did just hit me. I confronted him in the bathroom, yelling, "What in the world is going on here?" I yelled at him for not doing anything I asked and for everything he had put us through. I went in his room and picked up his huge wooden desk and smashed it against the wall. I'm never violent with anyone, especially my family, but I guess I just needed to do something to release my anger. Daniel started yelling back at me and then stormed outside to the front yard.

I guess Nicole called Barbara at the banquet to tell her what was happening. By the time Barbara got there, I had followed Daniel out into the yard and we were just screaming at each other outside. Barbara managed to calm us down, and I agreed to take a walk with Daniel. By that time, the period of rage had passed and I got myself back under control. On the walk I told him, "Look, I'm sorry. You know, I didn't mean to get so out of control. You just really got me going." He goes, "No, I get it, it's my fault. I know I've been a real jerk." And he keeps going on, apologizing, saying he's going to be better. He's going to move out, quit the drugs, get a job, and stop doing all of this to us. By the time we came back, we were okay. The next day he moved out.

After that, he was legally no longer living with us, and physically he was there much less. But emotionally, he was always there. It was like living on pins and needles because you never knew when he was going to call, when he would show up, when we would have to dish out thousands more dollars for another rehab or halfway house, when my wife would leave in the middle of the night to go look for him on the street. And that night before his emancipation was far from the first or the last time he promised he would quit. All the time he would come to us with these big speeches about how this time he was really ready to stop and things would be different if we would just wipe the slate clean. Barbara was always willing to give him more chances, but after a point I just couldn't take it anymore. It's like, if he's really gonna stop it's not enough to just tell us that; he's gotta actually do it. As soon as you start believing something he said, you would get let down. It was all talk, and eventually I was just tired of his lies. My opinion is that he knew my wife would always come through for him, so he didn't have much incentive to stop. A lot of the time, he was just manipulating her. She knows that's my opinion, and she disagrees, which is her right.

Maybe this all makes me sound like a bad person and a lousy stepdad, but it's how I feel. All I can say to someone who doesn't understand why I feel that way is, how about you let someone who is constantly delusional from using massive amounts of drugs live in the room next to your seven-year-old? Try having two stepchildren with addictions and a wife who is up all night every night bearing the pain of that and see how you feel.

The best way I can describe it is it's like you're speeding down a highway at 300 miles an hour with no brakes and headed for a dead end. As soon as you see an off-ramp, you find out it's closed. So you just have to keep wondering, what's going to happen once I hit that wall? Is anything going to give? Is anyone going to make it out? It was just a nonstop nightmare, nonstop.

Peter

Value

I think I did forty-five days in treatment the first time. One of my friends owned some townhouses and had a room for rent, so when I got out, I moved in with him. My dad agreed to pay half of my rent as long as I went back to school and was doing well. So, I started taking classes again and got a part-time job at a gym.

My best friend at the time, who I had been using with since high school, had also gone to treatment shortly before I did. A couple months after I got out, he died of an overdose. That was a big wake-up call for me. Of course, I knew that people die from the stuff I was doing, but that doesn't really sink in until it happens to someone close to you. I wasn't responsible for getting him started with drugs, and I knew that, but I also didn't help. So, I did feel shame for that, especially when I thought of his family. A lot of people who knew we were close called me, just wanting to talk about him, and I felt like I had to console them. It was a really tough time. But I think seeing that happen was a big deterrent for me for a while. I knew that I couldn't keep living the way I had been living, or the same would happen to me. In my former mind-set, I didn't really care about that. I didn't actively want to die, but I also didn't really care about preventing it. But in treatment, people had planted the seed in my head that my life had value, and now I wanted to protect that.

I went through the motions for a while and stayed clean, and it was nice to be independent and have my own space. I was doing what I was supposed to be doing, but I wasn't really happy. I kept going to NA meetings until I got my one-year chip and then decided I had enough of that.

When I was about to turn twenty-one, I decided I was going to go out drinking for my birthday. I didn't plan to start back on harder drugs, but I was tired of trying to stay sober and just wanted to live a normal life. I was drinking for a little while and doing okay, but then I starting hanging out more with a guy I met through *Magic*. I didn't realize it at first, but he was doing a lot of opioids, and I started doing them with him. At that point, it really became a conscious choice. I thought that if I started on drugs again, and went back to rehab, I could kind of get a reset. When I got out, I could get a different job, figure out what I really wanted to be doing at school, where I really wanted to live, and all that. I also don't think I had really processed my mental situation and my childhood, and I wanted to go back to do more therapy. I know now that I could have done all of that without going back to drugs, but in the head space that I was in, it made sense to me. And probably in the back of my mind I just wanted to use drugs again. I had been an addict for a long time.

I was doing drugs again for a couple months or so and saw the road I was going down. I had been there before, and this time I wasn't interested in playing the tape all the way to the end. I was ready to go back to rehab and work on things again. So, one day I just went over to my mom's house and told her what I was doing and that I wanted to go back to treatment. It didn't really seem to surprise her this time. I think she already had an idea of what I was doing. It was easy to hide the first time because no one even considered the possibility that I could be using heroin, but once everyone knew I was capable of it, it was a lot harder to keep that secret. Once you know what to look for, the signs become pretty obvious.

I went back to the same place for the second stint and knew what to expect, so it wasn't such a shock this time. I went to more therapy groups and just tried to absorb what I could and get my head on straight so I could get ready to be back on the outside. Once I got out this time, I went to a halfway house for about six months, went back to school for an English degree, and got a job as a server. I started dating someone and was working out and just generally felt healthier and like I could start living in a normal way. Working out and losing weight actually helped me stay clean because it was like a visual indicator of my progress. People noticed I was looking better and complimented me on it, so that gave me a lot of motivation and confidence. I had to go to more NA meetings in rehab but didn't continue once I got out. I know they're helpful for some people, but in the place I was at, it felt more like they were keeping me focused on the unhealthy part of my life. I was ready to move past that, and it was more helpful to just try to put more time and space between me and that lifestyle.

One of the biggest realizations I had was that children have very little agency, but adults do. When I was young, I had very little choice about what I could do with my life. When I was mistreated, there wasn't much I could do to fight back or get myself out of those situations. I dealt with it the best I could at that time, which was to just stop caring about myself. As I grew older, though, I gained the ability to make my own choices and resist anyone who told me otherwise. I realized that now I have the ability to forge my own path and I now have a desire to do it.

More than anything, recovery to me just means a lot of hard work. When you come out of rehab and try to start a new life, it's like you're starting in a hole. You have to climb up just to get even with everyone else your age, then you have to work two or three times harder to get ahead. My days were spent trying to balance work, school, and a healthy lifestyle all while trying to actually internalize and practice all the mental tools I had learned in treatment. Some people say that recovery is a miracle, and I understand why it can seem that way, but that's not how I see it. I don't think I got where I am now because of intervention by God, or because something amazing and magical happened to me. I got here through a lot of really hard work and discipline and sacrifice, and I have to keep working on it every day.

CHAPTER 6

Cycle

As difficult as it has been for me to accept, we can't change the past. I made a lot of mistakes with my children. We all do. The mistakes might have had good intentions behind them, but regardless of intentions, I have to accept the consequences. I think parents have to try to learn from those mistakes, forgive ourselves, and hope our children forgive our mistakes as well.

I still have a lot of trouble forgiving myself for things that happened when Daniel left home. After he was emancipated, I could not legally compel him to be anywhere he didn't want to be. There is a law in Florida called the Florida Mental Health Act, or "Baker Act," that allows adults to be involuntarily committed if they are deemed to have a mental illness and be dangerous to themselves or others. I invoked this many times with Daniel over the years, but the maximum holding period is just seventy-two hours after the person is stabilized. After that, sometimes they'll be sent to a mental health facility or enrolled in outpatient treatment. Other times, they'll just be released. Countless times, after he was released from an involuntary hold, I set him up with a friend or convinced him to go to a residential treatment center or a halfway house, but inevitably, he would soon decide he no longer wanted to be there and go off on his own. Soon after, without fail, I would get a call from him asking for money for food or clothes and other things that he left behind when he ran away.

If he didn't contact me after a couple of days, I became so scared that I couldn't sleep. On those nights, I would go out looking for him, driving through the neighborhoods I knew he frequented. If I couldn't find him, I would go home, wait by the phone, and ask the other women in TAM to please send him their prayers. If I did find him, I would buy him a hotel room for the night. If he was with someone who didn't have a place to sleep, he would beg me to buy a room for that person too.

Once Daniel started to see the realities of what people experienced living on the streets, he developed a lot of empathy for people who are homeless and became passionate about helping them however he could. Although there were stretches of time when he didn't have a place to sleep, he also knew he was fortunate to have a mother who was still so concerned about his well-being. He knew many people didn't have that. If he did have a little extra money, he would buy food for someone else. When he didn't have money, but did have a place to stay, he would fill up cups of clean water and bring them out to people on the street nearby. In short periods when he was sober, I would sometimes take Daniel to speak with other TAM moms, or local groups learning about addiction. He would always talk about what he had seen on the streets, about how sick some of the people are and how roughly they were treated by the police. He also wanted to highlight that he was proof that this could happen to anyone. He came from a family with money and had a mom who was willing to do anything to help him, and his addiction was proving to be more powerful than any of those resources.

Daniel's treatment-relapse cycles didn't last months, they lasted days. As the years progressed, I tried everything I could think of to help him. The most common advice I got was to cut off contact. People would say, "You need to stop enabling him; you're killing him," and I did try to take their advice. I would cut off contact for a few days at a time, and each time was a new nightmare. I would turn the phone off for a while until the not knowing became unbearable. Then I would turn it back on and just let it ring—at least hearing the ringing let me know he was still alive. Sometimes I would just go sit in our walk-in closet with my hands over my ears because I couldn't bear to talk to anyone. For the first time in my life, I started taking sleeping pills to fall asleep. If Daniel came by the house, Rudy would refuse to let him in. Can you imagine knowing that your child is living on the street and telling them they can't even come inside your house? That's what we did, and sometimes I still can't conceive of it.

I remember one time when I decided I was going to use "tough love" with Daniel and actually followed through with it. Several people had recommended that I try cutting off all communication with Daniel for thirty days. Maybe if I let him fall, he would finally figure out how to pick himself back up. So I moved in to our condo, where he couldn't find me, for a full month. It was the worst thirty days of my life up to that point. How could I sit there and do nothing knowing my kid is addicted to drugs, suffering from mental illness, and living out on the streets with nowhere to go? He couldn't even ride the bus when he was high because he would get kicked off. I honestly don't know how I made it through, but I did. That was in the fourth year of his eight-year addiction so, clearly, it didn't work.

The only time I could be sure that my son was off the streets was when he was legally mandated to a jail or locked mental health facility. In 2012, after being Baker Acted, Daniel was committed to the Florida State Mental Hospital. There were really strict rules on what kind of possessions the patients could have with them. I must have been more persistent than most families, because I eventually convinced the staff to let Daniel have a pencil so he could write. Daniel would get really anxious and agitated when he didn't know the time, so I also convinced them to let him have a watch. They said it couldn't be made of metal, so I bought a cheap rubber one. As a nervous habit, he started fidgeting with the watch and even chewing on it. I visited him there often; we would sit in the visiting area, and he would read to me from whatever book he was reading. Sometimes he would read from the Bible; other times it would be poetry or literature. His favorite books were always about a character who was having a really hard life. Whenever I visited, I would notice he had broken another piece of his watch. The band started breaking, then part of the clasp was missing, and then all of the paint was chipped away. By the day he was released, the band had fallen off completely, so the face of the watch was the only thing left, and he would carry it in his pocket. I asked him if I could have it. It was so sad to me. It showed how much he had disintegrated over time. He was falling apart. I still have that watch, and it's one of my most treasured items from Daniel.

Daniel regularly stole cough syrup from drugstores, and he took Rudy's cigars and alcohol from our liquor cabinet. He took drugs from our friends' medicine cabinets. He showed up at the house clearly intoxicated and yelled at me and Rudy. He lied to me and broke things. He would constantly lose the clothes and CDs and books I bought him, and I would buy him more. But looking back, none of those things really matter to me. When you're trying to survive and so many things are happening, things like that just seem so small. When you're looking at somebody who's dying in front of you, who's being forcibly committed by the police, who's getting incarcerated and hospitalized and held in mental hospitals, I couldn't care less what he stole. I was in survival mode. I just wanted him, and me, to survive. When you're an addict's mom, or an addict's sister, or daughter, or whatever, those things are so normal. You're so used to the abnormal.

The first time I went to a jail to visit my son, I felt so awkward and scared and disturbed. After a while, I didn't even have to think about the protocol. I learned exactly what to do and what to expect. It was normal to have to be searched. It would be normal to have to see my son through a window. It became normal to not be able to touch him. It was normal to have to talk to him through a phone. Sometimes the two of you aren't even in the same place—you're seeing each other on a TV screen. I'd drive hundreds of miles just to watch a video of him. Maybe that's the most horrible part of it all; so many horrible experiences became normal.

The first time Daniel was in an adult jail for an extended stay, I told him to look for the biggest, toughest inmate he could find that he felt comfortable approaching. When Daniel called me, I asked him to put that guy on the phone with me. I told the other inmate, "Hi, I'm Daniel's mother. I heard that you're a really tough guy and you help people in there. Daniel is really young, and I know if you were that young in there, your mother would want someone to protect you. If you can look after my son and watch his back if he gets into any trouble, I'll pay for your phone calls. Daniel and I talk on the phone almost every night, and you can use those times to talk to whoever you want."

Making calls in jail costs a fortune, and most of the inmates and their families can't afford to call regularly, so most of the men would take me up on my offer. Daniel would call me and then hand the phone to one of his protectors. Then I would make a three-way call to whoever they wanted and put down the phone so I wasn't listening in to their conversations. I racked up hundreds of dollars in other people's phone calls, but at least I could rest a little easier.

Once after he was released from jail, at perhaps one of my lowest points, I paid someone I knew to let Daniel work for him. Daniel would frequently say he wanted to get a job and support himself, and then would change his tune and say that the only job he wanted was to be a famous musician. I was fed up and hoped that maybe if he got a taste of the responsibility and structure a job required, he would change his attitude. No one would hire him outright with his history, so I asked my friend if he would give Daniel work to do on his carpentry jobs, and I would pay all of Daniel's wages. That "job" lasted two-and-a-half weeks.

Even now, looking back, I don't know how I can pull apart which of my actions were "right" and which were "wrong," when I went too far, and when I didn't go far enough. When was I helping and when was I hurting, even though it was never my intention to hurt anyone? I know that giving and caring for others has been integral to my personality from the beginning of my life. I was always the kid to organize group projects in grade school. When I was probably nine or ten years old, I remember waiting up for my father to get home from work and watching him and my mother get into a fight about something. My father was my hero at that time, so it would make me feel good to stay up with him and make him food or just listen to his troubles. When I was a young adult and found out my older brother was addicted to heroin, I would do anything that I thought might help him. When he got into treatment, I went to visit him frequently and brought him anything he needed. He got himself into recovery and has had a very successful life, and I would still drop everything if he really needed me. I have always been drawn to caregiving; I like being needed. That has always been part of my identity, and it is natural that it would extend to my son, who seemed to need me more than anyone. But when your teenage son grows into a young adult and is still stuck in a relentless cycle of addiction, treatment, and incarceration, what is a mother's natural, or "normal," response supposed to be? How do you determine what are healthy ways to deal with such an inherently unhealthy dynamic? I still can't say for sure.

Daniel just kept deteriorating and kept taking the pills to feel normal. But eventually his normal meant living in the world of his drug-induced hallucinations. When he was high, he would tell me he could speak three languages. He would tell me he was meant for some other world, that he could speak to God. Sometimes he would tell me, "I'm so scared, Mom. I want to quit, but what if I can't?" Other times, he would snap at me, "You just don't understand! The DXM takes me to a higher level of existence."

There was one unimaginable experience that stands out above the rest in my memory. It was nighttime, sometime in late 2014. I was awake in the bedroom and Rudy was sleeping next to me. The phone rang, and I took the phone out in the hall so I wouldn't wake Rudy. Of course, it was Daniel, and he sounded terrible. The more he tried to talk, the more incoherent he got. I could tell he was starting to pass out, so I started asking him, "Daniel, where are you? Look up Daniel, do you see any signs nearby? What are you wearing? What color is your shirt?" A few times he tried to mumble something, and he finally got out "Riviera Beach" and "Walgreens." I started screaming at him, "Daniel, I love you! Please stay awake," but he finally passed out. I got my other phone and called the Riviera police. I was hyperventilating as I tried to explain the situation to the operator, and she kept asking me to calm down so she could understand. She finally understood and sent the police to look for him. She stayed on the phone with me, asking for any details I could give her, the color of his hair, skin, eyes, his height, what he might be wearing. Eventually, she had asked and said everything she could think of and told me, "Ma'am, I'm so sorry, but I'm going to have to hang up until I have more information for you. The police have checked every Walgreens in the area and haven't found him yet, but they will keep looking and I'll call you back."

I waited by the phone for an hour, maybe the longest hour of my life. I knew he would die if they didn't get to him. The operator called back and said they had found him and rushed him to the hospital. He would survive, but next time he may not be so lucky. I had been through several overdoses with him before, but his addiction had progressed so far by

71

then and he was taking more and more pills to get the same effect. I just knew that he was dying.

■

Barbara

Contract

TAM Facebook post

I found a contract that I wrote and me and my son Daniel signed on February 8th, 2011, the day I took him back home to help him with his recovery.

My contract with my son:

Dear Daniel,

I think by now you know that I love you beyond words and that I am willing to support you to maintain a drug-free lifestyle. I pray you will have a responsible life filled with love, honor, and blessings. Therefore, I can no longer be a part of your life as a drug addict.

Today we start on a clean slate. As of today, you will be coming to my home. I will do everything to put your recovery first. I hope you do too. I am willing to provide you with outpatient therapy and an individual therapist and a psychiatrist. On your part, you have agreed to attend 90 meetings in 90 days. I believe in your ability to change. I also believe that you are not unique and, in fact, that it is very hard for you to be drug free. NO MORE EXCUSES. As we discussed, if you have a craving, you will tell me FIRST before you use. That will give us a few options (e.g., going to the hospital, attending a meeting, calling your sponsor, etc.). However, YOU WILL NOT USE or all bets are off. This is not a threat. I firmly believe that YOU ABSOLUTELY CANNOT CONTROL DRUGS. As you always say, one is never enough and 1000 is never too many.

The plan is very simple: if you use drugs you will be asked to leave my home. I will not have any contact with you until you have 30 days clean. This means you may have to get yourself into detox, a treatment center, or a halfway house that provides the structure you might need. I will provide the first three months of rent and food for you if you have the manager call me and tell me you are actively working a Twelve Step program, going to meetings, and you have a sponsor. However, if you get kicked out of the halfway house because you use, you will be on your own.

Leaving you on the street is the last thing I have ever wanted to do. It is the hardest thing in the world for me, and you too! However, I am not doing this to punish you. I am doing this in the most loving spirit. I cannot go on watching you die in front of me. YOU ARE NOT UNIQUE. You will have to work very hard to save yourself. I cannot do it for you, or love you into recovery. If I could, you would be 100% sober.

I pray we can work together, I pray it never comes to this. YOU, ONCE AGAIN, HAVE A CLEAN SLATE.

I love you with all my heart,
Mom

Daniel and I both signed this contract. Sadly, on the third day of being in my home, after putting $500 down on an outpatient rehab, he called me and told me he was leaving to get high. I did stick to my contract for the first time in my life. I did not speak to Daniel for 30 days until he had 30 days clean, which was in jail. I handed my phone to my husband and changed my phone number. Much has transpired since that day in February 2011. Tomorrow, Daniel is starting a new rehab, this time of his own doing. This time I pray he stays and finds recovery. The real high is no high. PRAYERS NEEDED.

Much love to you all . . .

(September 27, 2011)

Daniel

Journal Entry

Homeless in South Miami

In truth, I was not homeless for I only needed to call my mother who, although furious about losing the deposit on the halfway house, did not yet have the heart to leave me on the streets. My stay on the streets would last a night or two and I would inevitably call my mother and would go to whatever halfway house she placed me in.

And so I came across a grassy park and lay down under an oak tree. My iPod had not yet died so I listened to *The Dark Side of the Moon* under the psychedelic influences of DMX, staring wide-eyed at the sun.

Then I saw him, a homeless man also lying upon the grass and I began to wonder about him. Where had he lived? Where was his family? Why was he homeless? I imagined what it would be like to be that man. Always living on the beach, always lying on the grass, he was no longer a part of conventional life. And so I wanted to know what had happened.

I imagined him growing up as a normal child; I imagined he was just another kindergartner in the classroom. I imagined perhaps he developed schizophrenia, his parents had tried to get him counseling, medication, institutions. And maybe after all had failed they broke contact with him. Imagine the people from his youth walking past him as he panhandled on the streets, at first offering support and consolation and gradually recognizing him less as the years went by, and finally not at all. Imagine the tears of his first night on the street alone and forsaken.

Twenty years go by and here we lie upon the grass, and you are so foreign to me. What is it like in your shoes from the outside looking in? Picking from garbage cans, smoking discarded cigarette butts, watching the beach front waitresses enthusiastically calling daily specials to passersby. They do not call out to you though; you are what society denies, the man people pretend does not exist. Avoiding eye contact within their cars as you hold your cardboard sign, stepping over you as they walk down the sidewalk.

The people cannot look in your eyes; they are not brave enough to allow poverty, mental illness, and addiction to impede upon their productive conventional lives. You are no longer a consumer, and so all the attention and respect, kindness, and servitude provided by the working class to the consumers is not shown to you. I do not know you, and I never shall, yet you serve as a portrait of the casualties of American society. And I hope as you lie upon the grass with me perhaps you feel a peace, and know an enlightenment that we have somehow missed. In no hurry at all, lying in the grass in the sun.

(2011)

No Trust

Thinking about Daniel is hard for me for different reasons than why it might be hard for Nicole or my mom. By the time I moved in with my dad, Daniel was only about ten, so I wasn't super close with him growing up. I do have some positive memories of us playing video games together and things like that when we were really young, but I can't remember a ton from that time. When I think back, I mainly remember him as one more person who made my childhood difficult. I saw him as taking my mom's attention away from the rest of us, and since he had a hard time making friends, my mom tried to force me to include him in things. He didn't understand boundaries or a lot of social norms, and I didn't have much patience for that as a kid. He seemed to want attention from me, but only in a negative way. I thought of him as a chaotic force in our house.

After I moved out, I didn't have very frequent contact with him, and I don't think we ever went to school together. I had already been on the path of my destructive lifestyle for quite a while when my mom called me saying he had started on drugs and asking me if I knew about the stuff he was taking. I told her what I knew about Triple Cs, saying I had heard about kids using them at school, not saying that I had used them myself. I wasn't super shocked to hear he was doing it, since it was true that a lot of people at school were. But I was surprised by just how bad he got over time. I knew he had behavioral issues since when he was young, so I thought maybe we'd have to keep supporting him as an adult. He would probably get some low-level job and we might have to help him out financially, but he'd be basically okay. Obviously he took a much worse turn than I expected.

After I was out of rehab and relatively stable, his addiction was still in full force. I was living in a halfway house for a while, and my mom asked if he could come stay with me for a night or two so I could teach him some of what I had learned. I had a feeling it wouldn't go well and was reluctant, but I agreed. He came over, some of my housemates and I took him to an NA meeting, we got some food and then went back to the house. Basically as soon as we were back, he got high. He must have brought some of his drugs into the house. Getting high in a halfway house where a bunch of newly sober people are living is not only against the rules but is hugely triggering and dangerous for everyone. Needless to say, I was very upset with both him and my mom. I let her convince me to try it one more time later on, but the same thing happened. He couldn't keep it together for even one night when he was with me.

Sometime after that, I was staying at my dad's house for a few days and heard Daniel was also coming to stay over for the weekend before going to another rehab. I didn't trust him at all at that point, so I hid my laptop in my dad's room whenever I left the house. Things were fine for a couple days, so I got sloppy and left it out on the kitchen table before going out with some friends. When I came back, he had stolen it and run away. It was the day before he was supposed to go to rehab. I never asked what he did with it, but I assume he pawned it for more drug money. That was the last straw for me. It wasn't about the cost of the laptop—I had a ton of content on there that wasn't backed up. I needed it for school and all of my assignments were on there, everything I had written. He had proved time and time again that I couldn't trust him, he was showing no signs of actually wanting to get better, and he was harmful for my own recovery, so I decided I needed to cut him out of my life as much as possible. After that, I hardly ever saw or talked to him at all. Knowing that my mom was still so squarely in his corner didn't help my relationship with her either.

Barbara

Letter to Daniel

Dear Daniel,

There is a void in me, almost a hole that can never be filled with anything but fear and sadness while you are gone or not okay. Most addicts' mothers' hearts are broken and the decision to detach with love becomes the only decision left after countless attempts over many years are made to save her child. One day she looks around and stares straight in the faces of her loved ones and she sees so much hurt, sadness, and pain. She now realizes she MUST change. Not because she does not love her addicted child, but I and so many other mothers of addicts would give our lives if our addicted child could only be okay. But it is not realistic or possible because she knows that she is a mother, sister, daughter, friend as well as an addict's mother. The people who love her need her too. Especially her other children who need a mother who is not always crying, absent, or numbing her pain with alcohol.

Daniel, I pray you mean what you say—we are both torn up inside. You know my love for you is forever. You are a beautiful person and I truly love you. Losing you to drugs has been the saddest thing that has ever happened to me in my life. What I wouldn't give for you to be back as a productive member of our family and society. With each missed day the hole only gets bigger. I wake up each day with a stomach ache that usually lasts until 2 or 3 p.m. My mind wrestles, am I a terrible mother? The phone rings over and over, my hands are over my ears, tears are running down my cheeks, and my stomach is in a knot. I know it is you, you who I love so much, my beautiful son, but yet I let it ring and ring. I have made a promise to myself, and the rest of our family, that I will detach with love from you due to your lifestyle because it is literally killing me, and honestly even if I die what good would it do, to you or anyone else?

I am not going to go on and on about why you should stop. We both know the mighty cost of what you are doing to yourself and to those who love you so dearly. I forgive you, although I will not accept disrespect. I am too old to allow my children to behave in a disrespectful manner to me. In my eyes you will always be my beautiful child and, as I told you many times, God gives each of us only one mother and you must respect her.

Daniel, I have made some boundaries for both of us. You can call me when you have been sober for two weeks in treatment. When you have one month sober, I will come to see you.

When you get out of jail, I have arranged for someone to pick you up; we will figure out from there whether you can go straight to the treatment center. If that is not possible, you will be provided a safe place to stay until the next morning and then you will go to the treatment center. Also, I will get your belongings to you and at the completion of every week I will send you a new book. I am not sure what you need upon arrival, but whatever it is we will get it to you.

Daniel, I am not punishing you. You know I love you sooooooooooooooo . . . much. I am just older, sicker, and even somewhat wiser. I know I can't change you, only you can. To watch you destroy yourself is more than I am capable of, so I must change and stick to my boundaries for both of us.

With the utmost love and respect I am sending this to you. I love you, and I have always forgiven you. I will be praying for you and our family. Always keeping in mind the Prodigal Son, I will never stop praying for your return.

Remember to pray to God to help you. I truly believe you cannot recover without his help. May God help walk with you on your journey . . . As always, I pray for your return daily.

Love always and forever,
Mom

(July 27, 2012)

Daniel Worsening

When I moved away for college and it was clear Daniel wasn't improving, there were times when I would get really angry at my family. I was pre-med, working really hard toward a career, and trying to be very money conscious. I would turn down invitations to go out with my friends so I could save money and cook at home. Meanwhile, Daniel would go out and get high and lose his $150 Jordans that my mom bought him. He would promise that he was going to change this time, and she would just buy him another pair. She would constantly buy him new CDs, a new CD player, new books. I would get resentful at times, but I also tried to be empathetic. I would have to remind myself that Daniel was sick, Rudy was helping me a lot financially, and my mom was doing the best that she could. My mom told me that I couldn't really understand why she did what she did until I had kids of my own. At the same time, everything my mom was doing for Daniel didn't seem to actually be helping. Besides just the stuff and the money, he knew that if he left a treatment center or got kicked out of a halfway house, she would always find him another one. I would tell her that by always coming to the rescue she wasn't really giving him any motive to get better, but it was a continuous cycle. At certain points, my mom did try to cut off contact with him. If he couldn't reach her, he would call me. He really loved me, and sometimes he would call just to talk. But often he was high, and you never knew when he would call because he was in some kind of crisis.

During one of the periods when my mom wasn't answering, I was at a friend's house and got a hysterical call from Daniel. He was freaking out and crying on the phone, telling me that he had no front teeth and asking if I could come get him. I'll never forget how upset he was. I left my friend's house and cried in the car all the way home. I wasn't anywhere near him so I couldn't go get him. There was nothing I could do. I found out later that the police were arresting him, he resisted, and they hit him in the face with a baton and knocked out his front teeth. I went with my mom to his court date and saw him sitting there with the jumpsuit on, handcuffed, with his front teeth missing. It was awful. I remember it really struck me at that moment how big of a toll this life was taking on him. I never wanted to see my brother like that. He just wasn't the same person anymore.

I don't know how many times I tried to convince Daniel to really commit to turning his life around. He would say he really, really wanted to stop. He really wanted to stop but he couldn't, and he was afraid—he said he didn't want to live a boring, normal life. He didn't want a regular nine-to-five job. He seemed to think that if he stopped doing drugs, he would lose everything that made him unique. I kept trying to explain to him that there are other options. There are ways around a conventional life besides being a drug addict. But for him, it was like that was the only option. He was either going to submit to being a boring person like everybody else or he was going to do drugs. It got to a point where he only felt like himself when he was using DXM. When he was off it, he felt like he was nothing. He was always trying to get me to understand his perspective and support it, and I always listened. But it came back to the same thing. I would tell him, "Daniel, I love you, but I can't support what you do."

Eventually, it got to the point where he literally couldn't tell the difference between what he was imagining and what was really going on. Not just when he was high and having hallucinations, but when he was sober. Every time I'd talk to him and try to rationalize his decisions, he would think I was just saying I was better than him and that I was putting him down. He seemed to lose touch with reality in a big way. He didn't get why nobody understood him. He went from thinking that he was better than everybody else to being concerned that everybody thought they were better than him. It was just a constant paranoia and he always thought he was being misunderstood. It just got worse and worse and worse. Healthwise, he was also constantly complaining about stomach pains and being tired. There were times when he came over and he would sleep all day long. I assume his liver was completely shot. But mentally, either he was high and his mind was somewhere else, or he wasn't high and his mind was somewhere else because he was thinking about wanting to be high. It got to the point where there just was no more Daniel. Everything in his life revolved around the drugs.

Barbara

Birthday 2014

TAM Facebook post

An Open Letter to My Son . . .

Dear Daniel,

Daniel, you left treatment yesterday, April 12th, 2014, once again, with no place to go but the streets.

Tomorrow, April 14th, is my birthday. We had planned on celebrating it together—you, me, and the rest of our family, in fact the whole family was coming to my house. I thought for sure you would make it this time. You appeared to like the rehab you were at and seemed to be doing so much better.

I recall our conversation this past Friday, when you told me that you couldn't wait to see your sister and brothers and you were so excited to come to my house and celebrate my birthday with me and the rest of our family. You made sure to tell me that you were done using drugs. You told me very strongly that drugs had ruined your life. You went so far as to say you hated them.

You repeated over and over that you just wanted your family back. Well, Daniel, your family just wants you back too!!

This would have been the first time in seven years when we would celebrate a holiday or a birthday together as a family— by this I mean as our entire family intact (including you).

Sadly, once again this will not be happening.

Daniel, if you should see my post, please know how much I love you. It is the drugs that I hate.

Please find your way back into treatment.

God willing there will be many more holidays and birthdays to spend together.

Sending tremendous love to you, my beautiful son, praying that you find your way out of the darkness, into the light. . . .

Until then I will forever miss you,
Mom

(April 13, 2014)

Daniel

Poem

No Heaven

Life is pain
and if you're sleeping on the street don't think it can't rain
the night is so long and so cold
there's no blanket all your stuff's been stolen or sold
and your clothes are wet
calling up the homeless shelter no beds are left
it's hard enough you're just trying to sleep
shivering in sand behind the wall on the beach

Damn searchlight here comes the police
Passed me this time hope they don't catch me in the next sweep
And if you can't find me momma don't weep
it's just another lonely night on these cold streets

There's no heaven for a drug fiend
no heaven for a junkie
there's no heaven for the mentally ill
no heaven if you're forced to steal
no heaven if you pop pills
there's no heaven for a man on the streets
no heaven when you follow your own beat
no heaven when there's nothing to eat
no heaven if you don't have Nikes
There's no heaven if you can't believe
there's no heaven if you can't see
there's no heaven for me

I'm sorry mom

I think something in my mind is wrong

I keep singing the same old songs

I've been away for so goddamn long

and I did what you told me to I asked Jesus for a partnership

but I don't think he was hearing it

I can't sleep at night I'm sick

I keep waiting for my luck to change

ever since I took those Cs everything's changed

and it's the happiest I've ever been

I'm only happiest when I sin

some people were born to win

some people were born to lose that's it

it's the boy you rejected

the schizophrenic who's infected

what's the man in the alley injecting

I can't expect you to care

life is unfair

when that man overdoses and hears

I'm sorry son

There's no heaven for a drug fiend

no heaven for a junkie

there's no heaven for the mentally ill

no heaven if you're forced to steal

no heaven if you pop pills

There's no heaven for a man on the street

No heaven if you follow your own beat

no heaven when there's nothing to eat

no heaven if you don't have Nikes

There's no heaven if you can't believe

there's no heaven if you can't see

there's no heaven for me

(2010)

CHAPTER 7

Let Nothing Frighten You

One memory of Daniel I'll never forget was in March of 2015. I was staying in the hospital with my father, who was very sick. He ended up living another eight months or so, but we thought he could die any day. Daniel was in court-ordered treatment and seemed to be doing better than he had ever done before. He called me, wanting me to come see him, but I couldn't leave my father. Rudy and Nicole were there with me one day, and the man who owned the treatment center did us a huge favor and brought Daniel over to the hospital himself so he would be able to see his grandfather. Daniel looked better than I had seen him in a long time. He was in a long-term treatment center, and they were giving him anxiety medications that other centers had never given him because they were potentially addictive. He said he also really liked the counselor he was seeing there. Something seemed to actually be making a difference, and he had stayed in treatment and off DXM for about two months. When we went in to see my dad, Daniel told him that he shouldn't be scared of dying. He told him he was a good man, so he shouldn't be afraid of the afterlife.

After Daniel and Nicole saw their grandfather, the four of us went to sit down in the cafeteria. Daniel was reading a book and, twice, he silently looked up from his book and just stared at me in the strangest way. He was slightly smiling and it looked like he wanted to tell me something, and I asked him, "Daniel, what are you doing?" But he didn't say anything and just went back to reading.

Before he left the hospital, he gave me a notebook. The cover said, "Do Not Struggle against a Rushing Stream." Inside were three things. One was a picture he had drawn of me labeled "Young Happy Mommy." The second was a petition to God:

> God, I pray that you would send solace to my mother in this time of her father's illness. God please strengthen me so that I can remain stable, remove selfishness from my heart so I can give my mom support.
>
> Help her defeat the stronghold of anxiety in her life. Shield her from any demonic oppressions, and pour your wisdom upon her.
>
> Incline her towards faith and the Holy Spirit. Remove illness and worry, let her be spurred into doing healthy, wise things. Teach her your ways, and let her find reconciliation with those who she believes may have harmed her.
>
> Let her find knowledge and fear of the Lord. Set your angels about her.
>
> Forgive her the iniquities she commits in ignorance.
>
> Let the light evaporate the darkness, teach her also how to rest and cease from constant labor. Also expose evil, corrupting influences in her life.

Finally, there was a simple note to me:

Dear Mom,

Let nothing disturb you, let nothing frighten you. Everything passes away except God. God alone is sufficient.

Love your son,
Daniel

Before he left to go back to rehab, I gave him a long hug and told him, "I love you so much." Because I did, I loved him more than I could say.

Just a few days later, I found out he had run away from his treatment center. He had been sober for seventy-seven days at that point, which was his longest streak since he had gotten out of DJRF when he was eighteen. That day, one of the counselors told me that she was worried because he had started getting in fights with other people in the center. Then, another patient stole his shoes and Daniel went ballistic. For whatever reason, that triggered something inside him. He thought the staff would call the police, and he couldn't stand the thought of going back to jail, so he left. He texted me asking for money and I wired him $20. That was the last time I talked to him.

Days went by and no one heard from him. It was incredibly rare for him to go more than a couple of days without contacting me, so I was very worried. I talked to the mothers on TAM and they mobilized, calling rehabs, jails, hospitals, and shelters all over Florida and beyond. We made missing posters, and TAM members shared them all across the country. As the days went on with no word, I knew something was really wrong. I was so scared, I could hardly do anything, but my sisters on TAM did everything for me.

He had been missing eight days when I got a call from the police. I could tell from their tone that it wasn't good news. I told them I was home alone and couldn't bear to hear whatever they were going to tell me without someone with me. I made them hold while I used my other phone to call Rudy at work. He was in a meeting, so it took them a while to find him. The police and I were waiting in silence for twenty minutes before Rudy joined the call and I told them they could go ahead and say it. They told me that someone found Daniel's body in the Intercoastal Waterway. My son was gone.

Barbara

Forgive Everyone

TAM Facebook post

About a year ago, Daniel looked at me with these big, brown, sad eyes and said, "Mom, what will happen when you die? How will I live without you?"

I bravely answered, "Daniel, everything I ever taught you is inside you. If I die, you will have everything you need to know from me inside of you. You will be fine, you will shine."

Who would ever expect he would die first? Now I want to scream out loud, "Daniel how will I live without you?!" Well, I guess I will have to follow my own advice.

Daniel, you taught me so much. Many times, I think of things you taught me and I am able to move forward, to do what I consider to be the right thing. You taught me about Jesus, forgiveness, love, and even Macbeth.

Love you, Dan. Today I wrote a note asking someone to forgive me, even though it was tough and I believed they were wrong. I remembered you saying, "Forgive everyone, especially your enemies."

Dan, I pray I see you again.

I love you,
Mom

(April 30, 2015)

Nicole

Grief

Before Daniel died, he went missing. It wasn't strange for him to be out of contact for a few days, but when it got to about a week I started to get concerned. My mom thought something was wrong even earlier. She had given him some money before he went missing, and she kept telling me that usually when she gave in and gave Daniel a little money he would quickly be back to ask for more. She felt that something was off this time, but I didn't fully believe it. I was thinking, "Nicole, this has been going on for seven years now and this is just what he does. Fool me twice, shame on me."

When my mom started making missing posters and asking people to look for him, it started to feel more real. But what really got to me was a conversation with Peter. Peter hadn't been in contact with Daniel for a while at that point so it wasn't like him to get emotionally involved with whatever was happening with him. But when I talked to Peter about it, he said he had a bad feeling about this time. If Peter was concerned, I realized I should be too.

Shortly after that is when I got the call from my mom. I was living with two of my best friends at the time, and one of them had two friends visiting. It was late morning or early afternoon and I was just hanging out in the living room. I casually answered the phone, since my mom had been calling almost every day that week. I thought nothing of it.

I answered the phone and just heard her screaming on the other end. "He's dead, he's dead, he's dead!" I ran out and stood outside the door to our apartment listening to her screaming, "He's dead! They found his body in the ocean!" I've never heard anybody that upset in my life, and I would never want that person to be my mom. It was the most horrible experience, and I honestly wouldn't wish it on my worst enemy.

I was completely in shock. My first thought was, "I can't go home right now." I found out on April 6th, and my college graduation was scheduled for May 1st. I had finals in two weeks and I had already been accepted to Physician Assistant school, which was contingent on me taking my finals and graduating on time. I realized I just needed to get through this, or I would have to deny my acceptance to PA school and take a semester off, which would be taking a huge risk and completely derail my career. When I got off the phone, reality finally hit me. My brother was gone, and of course I had to go home. I had to just figure it out.

I called Peter, who was at the gym at the time. His immediate response was, "Oh my God. Oh my God. Nicole, book a flight. I don't care when or where it is, get a flight, I'll come get you. I love you. It's okay. I love you. I love you." He just kept repeating, "I love you, we're gonna be okay. I love you. Get a flight. Come home. I'll see you tonight."

After that, everything seemed to go wrong. I bought a plane ticket but my shoe broke on the way to the airport, and when I got there I realized I didn't have my license. I couldn't find it anywhere, so my best friend took me to the DMV to get a new one. I had to get a new license picture taken that day. I finally got a flight that got into West Palm Beach around 3 a.m., and Peter and his friends drove more than an hour to come get me. When I finally got to the house, my mom was a wreck. We were supposed to have a slideshow of family photos at the funeral, but she couldn't handle looking through our pictures, so I did it myself. The funeral itself was just as awful. I was sitting next to my dad, who I hadn't spoken to for a while at that point, and there was obvious tension between several members of my family who weren't happy with each other. I was frustrated that we couldn't put our issues aside for even this one day. I got up and spoke about Daniel, but I barely got through it. To be honest, that whole week just feels like a horrible blur.

I spoke with my professors to see if there was anything they could do to help me with the terrible timing of my finals. They were all really understanding, but the best they could offer me was to let me wait and take them next semester, which would mean I would have to reject my offer to PA school. That offer was the culmination of everything I had been working towards, and there was no guarantee that I would get in again if I waited. I just couldn't risk that. So, I flew home shortly after the funeral to study. I had one good friend who I studied with all the time, and she knew all about my situation and what I was up against. Before I found out he had passed, we already had a plan for how we were going to get through finals. When I got back, we just did our best to follow through on that. The first day we got together, I told her about everything that happened and got all my feelings out. She listened and was really supportive. After that, we both just understood that I needed to do whatever I could to get through this. I had to hyperfocus on studying so I couldn't focus on anything else.

I graduated college two weeks later. My mom, Rudy, Alexander, Peter, and my grandma all came to the ceremony and, in spite of everything, they all did a great job making me feel supported and proud of what I had accomplished. I was really grateful for that, but there was also that guilt in the back of my mind saying we shouldn't be celebrating me two weeks after my brother had died.

That summer was a really complicated time. PA school was starting three months after graduation, and I felt like that was my allotted time to work through my feelings the best I could so I could free myself to focus on school. I had the realization in college that I had struggled with symptoms of depression on and off throughout my life, which wasn't surprising given my family history. Now I know how common depression is, especially among young people in stressful professions, and I have a lot of friends who struggle with it too. That summer, and the first part of PA school, were probably the worst. Part of me wanted to just sit and grieve, and another part didn't. I had to work to save up money for school, and I also tried to keep myself busy doing things with my friends so I didn't have to think about it constantly. I didn't feel like I had time for formal counseling or anything like that. Two or three months after he died, I got a tattoo that says "R.I.P. Daniel" on my ribs, under my heart. My mom was always against tattoos, so she didn't want me to get it, but she approved once I explained why I wanted it. I had started getting really nervous that my memories of my brother were going to fade over time. At the time, I had a close group of friends who knew Daniel, and I could talk to them about him and know they would understand. But I realized that every person I would meet after that would not know him. He would only be a story—I could talk about it, but no one would fully understand if they didn't know him. That upset me, so I figured that a tattoo would be a way to always keep him in my life. Daniel had several tattoos, so I think it is a good way to represent him. I like that people ask me about it, and I like that it's just a part of who I am now.

When I started school, I had really bad nightmares for a while. I knew they were connected to the grief, but I didn't have any option other than to get through it, so I did. It was also tough because, starting a new school, I was around a lot of new people every day. After I got accepted to the PA school several months before, a lot of people in my class started adding me on social media. My class was small, so when he died, word spread around. That period was hard. I didn't feel like people were judging me for my brother's addiction, but it was clear everybody knew and some people didn't know how to act around me. I was meeting all these great new people, and I wanted them to know me as more than the girl whose brother just died. It was just overwhelming.

There is still a lot of stigma about addiction and mental health disorders out there, and I know that makes a lot of people feel shame about having a family member who has an addiction. But I never felt that way. When I was younger, maybe it was because of how open my mom was with us about drugs and her family history; I don't know. Then, in PA school, I did a psychiatry rotation and learned about addiction and mental illness from a professional perspective. Addiction and mental illness are medical problems. People get sick in many different ways, and that's just one of the many ways. It's not anything shameful. I've been lucky because I haven't met many people ignorant enough to think less of me because of my family history, but if I do, I know that's not someone I want to hang out with anyway.

Turning Point

The last time I saw Daniel was not long before he died. My grandfather on my mom's side, Leon, was really sick and in hospice care, and a bunch of us went to see him. I actually had a lot of respect for my grandfather, and we had a pretty good relationship, so seeing him dying was really hard for me. Besides being emotionally on edge, I hadn't been talking with my mom much at the time. It was also my first time in a while being around some members of my extended family who I felt hadn't done anything to help my family when we needed it. Social convention said we were all expected to sit around and talk to each other like we were all good friends, and I just couldn't pretend like that. So, I was trying to just ignore everyone and stay focused on seeing my grandfather. My mom kept pushing me to talk to her, and eventually, I snapped and started yelling at her in the waiting room. Then Daniel walks in and he looks terrible. He had dyed blond hair with dark roots, had tattoos everywhere, was super pale, and had big dark circles under his eyes. It looked like he hadn't really slept in a long time.

I looked at him and actually thought, "This may be the last time you see him; you should go say something." Not just because he was in such bad shape, but because I hadn't seen him in so long, it would have made sense to talk to him. But I was having such a terrible day and was in such a bad place, the other side of my brain was like, "No way I'm talking to him." I went against my better judgment and just did what was emotionally satisfying at the time, which was to continue to ignore him. I think he could tell just from my body language that I didn't want to be approached so he looked at me, but didn't come up to me, and just sat on the other side of the room. We didn't talk that day, and it was the last time I saw him. Not saying anything that day is actually still a big regret of mine.

When I heard Daniel was missing, and when no one heard from him for several days, I knew something was wrong. I hadn't talked to him in a long time but I knew his patterns, and I knew that if he hadn't contacted anyone to ask for anything for more than a few days, that was a huge red flag.

The day of his funeral was a whirlwind. There were a ton of people at the ceremony, way more than could fit in the small room at the cemetery. People were standing in the back and some were out in the hall. Everyone was trying to talk to me, including a lot of people I wouldn't have wanted to talk to even under good circumstances. I had an assigned seat near the front, but Alex and I wanted some personal space, so we sat together near the back. I was surprised to see that a lot of my friends came. I didn't even tell them, so I'm not sure how they found out about the funeral, but I was really grateful for that. The hardest part for me was watching my mom have a full-blown breakdown. I don't even know how to describe it, and I try not to think about it, but she would try to speak for a while, and then ask others to speak and would just stand there touching them. Then she would take the mic from them or just start breaking down crying. I could tell she was experiencing so much emotion at once, and I felt it coming off of her. Despite all of the issues my mom and I have had in our relationship, it's terrible to see someone you care about clearly being in so much pain and not being able to control it. I really empathized with that because I've had similar feelings a lot in my life.

I just tried to keep to myself and get through it as silently and stoically as I could. Of course, it also crossed my mind that this funeral could have easily been for me. I had been in a few near-overdose situations, and it hadn't been long since I had seen this happen to one of my closest friends. Also, despite the fact that my relationship with Daniel had been largely negative, I had felt a connection with him. I knew we could relate to each other on a certain level that our other siblings didn't understand. Being the two oldest, and both being targets for hostility, we had a lot of similar experiences growing up. When you and another person share a similar experience of trauma, there is a bond between you. We just never had a productive conversation about it while he was alive. By the time he died, I had gotten myself to a pretty stable place. I was working and had good friends and my own place and had things to live for again, so, regardless of what I was feeling, I didn't let it throw me off course.

Daniel's death was really a turning point in my relationships with my family. I think it really caused all of us to reevaluate how we were treating each other. We realized we all needed support, and we needed to tread lightly. Now, I regularly keep in touch with everyone in my immediate family. Nicole and I talk about whatever's going on in our lives, and I'm glad she's doing so well. I'm disappointed that I wasn't there for Alex when he was growing up as much as I could have been, and I wish we could see each other more now. But we do talk and we have a good time when we're together. He seems to be avoiding the mistakes I made. I can't lie and say I've fully forgiven either of my parents for how they contributed to, or failed to prevent, the ugliness of my childhood, but I've gotten a lot better at dealing with my feelings and knowing my limits. My relationship with my mom has improved a lot. I think we both realized how bad things had really gotten between us, and we both wanted to change that. So, we now talk regularly and are much kinder to each other. I try not to live in the past and also recognize that going home often takes me back there. So, I have learned my boundaries and how not to put myself in situations that are going to bring out the worst in me. I pick up the phone when I want to pick up the phone, and I know when I need to keep things light. It's still definitely an ongoing process for all of us, but everyone is trying now, and my relationships have come a long way.

Daniel

Letter to Myself

Dear Daniel,

When you were young, a lot of kids made fun of you because you were different. I know how hard you tried to fit in. I'm starting to remember sitting with the kids in your class knowing that they really didn't care about your opinion. I remember those bullies calling you gay. I remember internal suspension. I remember the time your teacher said you were the most hated kid in class. I remember that bully beating you up, and the other kids saying you deserved it and Nicole crying. So many of those kids made you feel inferior. But you know what, you are special, and loving, and you are very important. Remember all the people who love you. You are no worse than them. God made you just as you are! So, don't sit there with them. Find people who won't judge you. You have an opinion that should be respected. And be who you are, don't change for anybody, and don't ever think you're dumb. Your dad criticized you, kids bullied you, but you are normal. Probably even smarter than normal. YOU ARE JUST AS IMPORTANT AS ANY OF THOSE KIDS. You are in honors classes, you have a loving heart, your family loves you so much!

Don't do drugs, please, it will ruin you. You will just be escaping. Your time is valuable. Work out! Do good in school! What they think doesn't matter. Be as good as you are.

Much love,
Daniel

(2009)

CHAPTER 8

The New Normal

For eight years, my thoughts and my life were consumed by the fear that the worst possible outcome would happen to me: my son would die. I did everything in my power to prevent that outcome at all costs. And in the spring of 2015, it happened anyway. My feelings have evolved over time—maybe that's me going through the stages. But the one thing that is undeniable is that my sense of self, and my "normal," has been changed forever.

I know a lot of people attended his funeral, including a lot of mothers from TAM who I had never even met before. I know we hosted some kind of gathering back at the house afterward. But if you were to ask for details, I couldn't give them to you. I can't tell you who exactly was there, or what the ceremony was like, how it was planned, or what I said. I was so numb that I can't remember any of that, if I ever absorbed it in the first place. I think Rudy and my ex-husband did most of the planning, but I'm honestly not sure how it got done. I know some parents do all of that without help, and I really don't know how they do it. I guess they just do it, because it has to get done. I guess I'm lucky I had the luxury to not have to figure that out.

If I had to summarize the time since then, the first year was mostly just that numbness. Maybe devastation. I didn't want to do anything but isolate. I didn't want to leave the house. I didn't want to talk to anyone. I didn't want to answer the door or the phone. When Rudy's business partner got married I couldn't, or wouldn't, go. I didn't want people to ask me about Daniel, or how I was. I realized there was no way I could manage TAM, and I was scared what was going to happen to it. But other mothers swooped in almost immediately and assured me that they would handle everything. They took over all the admin responsibilities and managed all aspects of TAM for quite a while. We received food and cards and flowers from people I barely knew almost every day for months. Some of the mothers wrote thank you cards for me. I had no idea how many people loved or cared about me until Daniel died. I couldn't manage myself, let alone an online community, but there was a lot of comfort in knowing I didn't have to.

At some point my primary emotion transitioned to a constant fear and dread. I was scared to live, scared to wake up, always scared that some other awful thing was going to happen. It's this impending sense of doom. Something is always very wrong, but besides the obvious, you can't put your finger on what it is.

Time is supposed to make it easier, but for me so far, it has made it harder. Maybe that's a result of the particulars of Daniel's situation. In the beginning, mixed in the mess of emotions, was a small sense of relief. At least my son wasn't suffering anymore. His life was so tragic for so long, and at least no one is able to bother him anymore. But over time, I started to miss him more and more. I started to realize how not normal it is for my son to be gone, and that I'm not the same person anymore. There was a part of me that was now empty and I was just going to have to get used to it.

Now, I have to consider that, for some people, living in this world is not always better than dying. I would love to see Daniel again, but I know that's a selfish feeling. I know now that there are some people who suffer so much more than others, and that's just a reality of this world we live in. Life was so brutal for Daniel that maybe it's better that he's free of it now. I see the pictures and stories of children who are locked in solitary confinement for years and years, who are subject to condemnation and abuse every day, who are constantly living on the brink between life and death, and I wonder if it really would be better for him if he were still alive. Was my unending desire to save him really for him, or for me? Was there ever a possibility that his story could be different? Of course, I have thought of every little thing that I could have done different. I wish I could say I was the perfect parent and was confident that all my choices were right, but I can't. I was the founder of an online community of mothers who bent over backward to help me and my son. I have a master's degree in family therapy. People will sometimes ask me if what I learned for my degree helped me deal with my sons' addictions. Honestly, I don't know. There is a world of difference between learning something in a classroom and implementing it with your own children. When you are struggling for day-to-day survival, I can tell you that you aren't usually thinking about what you learned in a classroom years ago. "Besides," I would think, "shouldn't my gut instincts as a mother, who has spent years of her life with her children, hold more weight than some theory from a textbook?" I had every advantage and I still can't honestly say that there even was something anyone could do to help Daniel. I'm not even sure if he had the power to help himself.

Maybe some people are meant to be here for only twenty-three years. Maybe God, or the universe, or whatever you believe in, has a plan and a role for all of us, and Daniel's role was to be here for as long as he was and impact all of the people and places that he impacted. I think I have to believe that. Despite all of his suffering, he was here and he had a tremendous impact on me, and on his family, on his friends, on everyone he met, and everyone who has and will read the pieces of himself that he willingly shared without any shame. For almost three years, I couldn't set foot in Daniel's room. Now, whenever I go in there I feel that Daniel is blessing me.

There's a certain profound sadness that I think all mothers who lose children live with. I think when you go through the worst thing that could ever happen to you, there are a lot of things that don't matter anymore. There are things that would have consumed me in the past that, now, I just can't bring myself to care about. Now that I have firsthand knowledge that the worst things in life really do happen, I engage less with the complicated and stressful little battles that I used to let eat away at me. I have an entirely different perspective and life has a different meaning. I don't attach myself so much to outcomes anymore. It doesn't really matter if something turns out the way I wanted; it matters that I did everything I could with what I knew at the time and that I tried to act with love and kindness, because that's the best that I can ever do. I've come to realize that I can't say, "I'm never going to achieve anything ever again because I lost my child" or "I'm never going to live again," because then I'm not valuing Daniel's life, or my life, or the lives of all of the other people I love. I have to value whatever time I have left and use that experience to make some kind of difference, if I can, and I need to protect what I have.

■

Letter to Alexander

Dear Alexander,

I have loved you dearly from the time you were born. And even though I may have teased you at times, I never meant to hurt you. Alex, in you is purity, in you is innocence, in you is kindness, and in you (most importantly) is compassion and emotion. I hope you believe me when I say that being apart from you has been perhaps the hardest thing I've had to endure these past four years. After a lot of thinking, I've decided that I will not move—in large part because I would like you to have a brother and a friend to encourage you and to let you know that you are very special.

But Alex, I have not been a very good brother, it's true. Having fun and getting high became even more important to me than you were. Alex, there is really no excuse. I was selfish and that's the truth. But there is still time for us to have a wonderful relationship! Alex, life can be amazing for you. Enjoy life, and do the things that fill you with passion! Follow your dreams, and never let anyone tell you that you can't make them come true. Also take your education seriously, because knowledge is valuable, and the more knowledge you have the better you will succeed in life. I regret not taking my school life seriously.

Alex, when you love yourself, guess what? No one can put you down. You don't have to live trying to be cool or accepted— the greatest men dare to be different. And so I hope you know that I am very sorry for all the things I've done, and God willing, me and you can forge new memories together. Also, you and I are brothers, we are not stepbrothers. I love you no less than Nicole or Peter. I have never thought of you as a stepbrother.

Alexander, may life be a blessing to you. May you find happiness, and love, and fulfillment. That's my wish for you. Lastly, never allow the cruelty of life to embitter you, or take your innocence, or kill your kindness. Alex, one of the greatest truths in life is this: love everyone, be kind to everyone, be generous, and be creative.

Love, your brother,
Daniel

(2012)

Don't Let It Stop You

I was really young when we found out Daniel was using drugs, I think eight years old. I remember him arguing with my mom, saying it wasn't a big deal and that he wasn't going to keep doing it. And I remember my dad being pretty angry that he was using drugs around me—Daniel's room was right across the hall from mine. After that, the whole situation started causing a lot of stress for everybody. He just kept making bad decisions that had consequences for everyone, not just him. My mom, and the rest of us, kept having to pick up his messes.

My mom would always be going to jail to try to get him out, or talking to the judge to get a better sentence. Or she would be sending him money or taking him to a motel so he didn't have to sleep on the street. I remember one time I found orange juice sitting out in the kitchen that had a purple tint to it. I didn't drink it, but I could have, and I didn't realize until later that it was juice mixed with a lot of cough syrup.

I didn't get much of a chance to know Daniel outside of his addiction. He was out of the house by the time I was nine, and most of the time when he came back he would just be causing problems for my parents. I do have a few good memories of him. One time he took me out for ice cream, and another time he took me to Kabooms, this cool arcade and restaurant, and we had a great time. Those little moments when he came home and seemed good, it was cool to hang out with him. But I could tell, near the end, that he wasn't the same person anymore. When things were really bad with Daniel, it was harder to focus on school and my grades weren't great. I remember in high school we had to keep our grades at a certain level to have a parking spot, and mine fell a little below that. But my mom went and talked to the school administrator to tell them what was going on, and they let me keep it.

Sometimes I would feel annoyed or frustrated about what we had to do for Daniel. Sometimes we would go to visit him in jail and I wasn't allowed in, so I had to sit outside and wait for everyone. But I never felt like my mom was neglecting me. She was always there for me when I needed her. I knew she was just doing what she had to do. I know she's always in my corner. My dad can be tough sometimes, but I know it's only because he cares. He's been by my side all my life. They both did their best to give me a normal childhood.

Ultimately, I think going through all that with my family made me stronger as a person. I think it made me better at problem-solving, and I'm pretty good in a crisis. Things in my life are a lot calmer now. I started working on cars with my dad, and I started a business detailing cars when I was fifteen. I'm still doing that, and am going to college. I have a pretty good relationship with Peter and Nicole—now that I'm older, we talk to each other more about our lives. I've never wanted to start drinking or try drugs because I don't want what happened to Daniel to happen to me. If there's anyone else out there going through similar things with their family, I'd say they should just try to stay strong and continue doing what they're doing. Try to help the person when you can, but don't make yourself constantly vulnerable. Try not to let it affect you too much, and don't let it stop you from doing the things you want to do with your life.

Daniel

Letter to Nicole

Dear Nicole,

Wow, I am proud of you! You have grown up so much and now you are in college, that's amazing! Nicole, you're a truly individual person. You are very special and brave. You may not think you are, but you are! You are a beautiful girl and most beautiful girls seek money and appearances, but not you.

You dated that guy because you liked his personality and character. And although you could have befriended the popular kids, the friends you have chosen have always been intelligent, funny, and unique—people with character. And you were impartial to their appearances and status. You have so many great qualities—you are intelligent, attractive, outgoing, charismatic and passionate. But you should know that perhaps your greatest quality is your kindness and your friendship to those people who much of the world would consider out of your league.

Listen, the truth is there is no excuse for my actions these past years. I was selfish, addicted, but also indulgent and apathetic to the people I should have cherished the most. But you know what? You and I have many years to have a wonderful relationship!

Nicole, you are fortunate because out of all of our family, I know that you will succeed in love and in life. Lastly, never allow life to embitter you or take your innocence or kill your kindness. Nicole, among the greatest truths in life: love everyone, be kind to everyone, be generous, be different, and be creative.

With your character and intellect, it's only a matter of time before you rule this world!

Love,
Daniel

(circa 2011)

Nicole

Balance

I'm at a good place in my life now. Things were very difficult for a long time, and it was sometimes a struggle to deal with Daniel's problems taking so much of the focus and energy within my family. There were times I felt I was on my own. But I really don't have a lot of resentments toward my mom or Rudy or my brothers. I won't say I'm happy that I had to be so independent, but I do think it taught me a lot. I was the youngest person in my program at school, and now I'm twenty-five and have already been working in my chosen career for a year. I've accomplished a lot, and I think part of that does stem from the fact that I learned how to handle things on my own when I was young. I think there's a difference between having to do things on your own and me knowing that, when it really came down to it, my mom would have dropped everything and come to help me if I really needed her. I knew that. I just didn't really need that, and other people did.

As I get older, I think I'm getting more and more similar to my mom. Now that we're both adults, I think she has let herself be even more open with me. She's always my mom first, but we're also best friends, and we have very similar personalities. People say we even talk the same way, which makes sense since I talk to her almost every day. Most of the qualities we share are positive, or neutral. The only negative I can think of is we both share a tendency to fall into relationships with people who need us more than we need them. I've learned that from some of the guys I've dated. But I'm learning to recognize it and set better boundaries.

I do want to have a family someday. I definitely want to be close to my kids like my mom is. I like how honest she was with me when I was a kid, and that we are still very honest with each other today. I talk to my mom about everything, and I always have. I do think that openness between us helped me stay out of trouble, because I never felt like I had to hide things from her.

I will say though, I don't want to have four kids like she did. I'd say two kids will be plenty for me. Statistically, with my family history, it just seems like having four kids is a bad gamble. And financially, emotionally, that's just a lot to take on. I know that even having one child can take a big toll.

Outside of my job, the one thing I can never sacrifice for my self-care is setting aside time to exercise. It's the best thing for my mental state. I also make an effort to stay connected to my friends. Having good, understanding friends has been one of the main things that has gotten me through the difficult times in my life. I've reached a point where I'm finally done with school and have a stable job. I'd like to find some more hobbies that fulfill me. I feel like my entire life I've been working toward getting where I am now with my career. Now I'm here, and I need to start working on everything else.

When I look back on the eight years of Daniel's addiction, I can't say whether everything I did was right or not right in the moment. But I do feel that I did everything I could to be a good sister to him. I can feel good knowing that I never completely abandoned him and never tried to make him feel bad for who he was. There were times when I had to set my boundaries, and I made it clear that I didn't support his decisions, but he knew that I never stopped loving him.

I think that's what I want to emphasize to anyone going through something similar in their family. Addiction is such a complicated situation, and there's no black-and-white answer to how loved ones should respond. You never know what's going to happen. There are people like Peter who get addicted to the most dangerous drugs and are able to work through it and do great things. Then there are a lot of people who never do, as hard as they try. You can never know what's going to happen in the case of the person you love. But through it all, you have to do what you feel is right and what's healthy for you. Personally, I know that if I had completely cut Daniel out of my life I would now be living with that regret and that would cause me a lot of pain. So, I would say, you need to try to find that balance between what is going to leave you with a good conscience and what you need to do to care for yourself. Know what lines you are willing to cross and which ones you aren't. Know that you can be there as a sibling or a mom or a dad without being harmful and without forgetting that you also matter. After everything, at least I can know that I did my best. Daniel knew that I couldn't support his addiction, but that I would always be his sister.

My family and I have had a very hard life, and everyone knows it. But I feel like when you have a hard life, there are two things you can do with it. You can either use it to be your main motivator, or you can use it as a crutch. I've just never wanted to use it as a crutch. I also know how lucky I was to have a good support system to help me through everything. Growing up, I didn't know many people who were going through quite the same thing as I was, and maybe having more of those relationships outside my family would have been helpful. But I did have a lot of great friends who did an amazing job supporting me, and I'm really grateful to them. Since Daniel passed, I have connected with a few people who were going through similar things with their siblings. In those cases, it has been nice to be able to talk to them and support them and even sometimes get help for them through my mom and her resources.

I feel like what I went through with Daniel had more positive lasting effects than negative. He influenced the career I chose, and, because of him, I have a lot of empathy for my patients with mental health problems. I care about them and connect with them in a way that most people don't. Sometimes I do see situations at work that remind me of him or my family, but rather than making me upset, it just gives me more motivation to do what I can to help them. I'm also good at emotionally detaching myself from my work when I need to. I can be fully present for my patients in the moment, but when I leave, I don't need to dwell on it.

Sometimes, as I'm going about my life, I'll see signs of him. Every once in a while, Daniel will show up in my dreams. And whenever something weird happens, I wonder if it's him. For example, a few weeks ago at around 3 or 4 a.m., my college degree fell off my wall and smashed to pieces. My cat flew off the bed. It was out of nowhere. I thought, "It's gotta be him messing with me." You know, there are just little things that have no explanation, and you wonder.

The Little Things

Take care of yourself first. If I have one thing to say to anyone who is dealing with all the stuff I did, that's it. Take care of yourself first. If you don't, it's like you're trying to drive drunk. If your life is constantly in a state of turmoil and you're not able to remove yourself from it and think objectively, how are you supposed to make sound decisions?

That's easier said than done when you're in a situation where the addicted person in your family is knocking on your door at two or three in the morning, but you have to figure it out. Barbara and I own a condo about an hour away, and we never gave Daniel the address. We used that as a kind of sanctuary when we had time to get away. I know most people don't have a luxury like that, but I would say you gotta do whatever you can to give yourself time and space to recharge your batteries. When I couldn't talk to my wife, I had a couple good friends and some family in Greece I would talk to about the situation. It's important to have a support system.

Today, Barbara and I are in a very different phase of our lives. Alex is a teenager and is pretty independent; it's not like he wants to spend too much time with his parents anymore. We spent so many years being caretakers, and it was intensive, concentrated caretaking. I still want everyone to do well and want to make sure they're okay, but now, we're looking forward to focusing on the simple things. I like to travel, and I go back to Greece three times a year. But when I'm traveling, I don't like to go sight-seeing or any of that tourist stuff. I like to just relax, have some good food, maybe go for a hike in the mountains. Alex usually goes with me once a year so I can show him the culture and the two of us can spend quality time, and then sometimes Barbara will join us for the end of the trip.

When I'm home on the weekends, I wake up in the morning, have a cup of coffee, watch the news, go out to dinner, take a walk. Maybe we'll go see a movie. I like to do things that are relaxing and give me energy, things that don't take a lot of effort. Soon, I want to start working less—drop down to three days a week. I don't want to stop working, because then you just sit around and get bored. But when you make things complicated, it shows up in your body, in your health. You learn that late in life, later on down the line, but you do learn it. Whether you accept that lesson or not is up to you, but I've learned that the best things in life are simple.

When it comes to my wife, the thing I love most about Barbara is the same quality I find the most challenging, because I've seen the negative impact it has had on her time and time again: She sees the good in everybody and she cares too much about everyone. It's a double-edged sword, and it depends on what side you're on. I love it when that care is aimed at me, obviously, but when it's on everyone else I can think, "Enough already, you can't save the world," you know? At the same time, I'm proud of her. She has helped a lot of people with The Addict's Mom, and I'm proud to be her husband.

Peter

Find Your Mission

Since I started to realize my value and turn my life around, my overall life philosophy has changed a lot. My physical health is important to me, so I try to work out and eat well and avoid things that are going to be harmful to me. I also have much better coping skills and tools to use when I encounter problems. Now that I've adjusted my attitude and perspective on life, I'm encountering fewer problems in the first place. But when something does happen, I try to think logically about how to solve it. Or, if I have a strong feeling about something, I try to break down the feeling and figure out where it's coming from and how to fix that root cause. I've also found that it's really important for my own well-being and self-confidence to give back to the world. One way to do that is to share my story with people who may benefit from it. I live in a small town and work from home, so I'm not having conversations with new people very regularly. But when I do get to know someone new, I'll usually only share the darker details of my past if I think it will be helpful for them. If it seems like they're going through something and need some hope or inspiration, I can tell them that I went through something really difficult, got through it, and am now trying to do something positive with my life. If my experience can maybe prevent someone from having to go through as much as I did, then I can find value in even the hardest parts of my past.

I've discovered that one of my biggest passions is to help animals. I've always felt connected to animals, and, unlike with people, you never have to worry about their intentions. When you are dealing with animals, you pretty much know what you are going to get and you know what they need. They are living, breathing, feeling creatures, and a lot of the time when they're in a bad situation, they aren't able to help themselves. In a way, taking care of them is a way for me to heal from the times in my childhood when I felt just as helpless. If I can give some safety and happiness to beings that otherwise have very little agency, that gives my life a lot of meaning. Right now, I have several pets and I volunteer at the Humane Society. My long-term goal is to buy a house with a lot of land and run an animal rescue. Maybe it sounds cliché, but knowing that others, including my animals, are relying on me gives me a reason to live. If I start using dope again, or fall back into my unhealthy patterns, I'll be letting down a lot of other beings and I won't be in a situation to help anyone. I'll be throwing away all of the progress I've made and all of the good that I'm trying to do.

It's hard to summarize all the things I've learned that could help someone who may be in the same place that I was ten or fifteen years ago. There's so much that I wish I could just make people suddenly understand, like when Neo learned kung fu in *The Matrix,* but there's no shortcut to growth. I've grown and developed the image of the person I want to be by harnessing and learning from every difficulty I've experienced. Sometimes, I'm only able to trust in something new after I've banged my head against the wall so many times that the old way gives me a headache. Other times, I'm able to learn from the headaches of others around me.

If there's anything I can impart to a person in early recovery, or who is still struggling to find recovery, it's that you have the ability to forge your own way, to determine the path you will walk. If you want to improve your life, the way I've found to get there is through a lot of self-discipline and practice making better choices. For a while, I had convinced myself that treating myself poorly was a way to get back at the people who have mistreated me in the past. But eventually I realized that way of thinking was only keeping me stuck in a destructive lifestyle. In reality, even if others do feel sympathy for you, they will eventually move on with their own lives. In the end, you are the only one who will have to live with the consequences of your own actions. So, I urge you to make decisions that will make your life worth living, whatever that means for you.

When your self-worth is at zero, or even below that like mine was, it's really difficult to treat yourself with dignity and respect. To find a compelling reason to make positive changes in my life, I had to look outside of myself. I had to find a cause that would make me want to keep moving forward at the times when I couldn't find the strength to do it for myself. For me, I discovered that my cause was to help animals. I could spend my income on pet food and vet visits, help homeless animals find a family, or contribute to getting stray cats spayed or neutered. If I ever feel the urge to go back to my old lifestyle, I try to focus on the ways I can help other beings and remember that I can't do any of that if I'm spending my time and money getting high. If I give up on myself, I also give up on anything good I can give to the world. In other words, if I don't see the value in myself some days, I can always find value in my mission. Find your guiding light and you will never get lost in the darkness.

Daniel

Live for Your Family

Dear Mom,

I know I don't express this often enough but I just wanted you to know that I really appreciate you. The amount of selfless effort you put into my recovery is allowing me to succeed thus far. Today, I just wanted to thank you so much for always being there for me. Hopefully one day I will be able to return the favor and be there for you in a time of need. I also wanted to apologize for my selfish behavior these last months. I felt like five days ago in the hospital I really had some kind of moment of clarity. I really feel as if I have a shot at staying sober off this cough medicine. To explain the amount of guilt I feel for everything, this is a burden I live with daily. In fact, there is not a moment I don't regret the people I have lost due to my addiction. I think about the countless relationships. I just wanted to let you know that I do recognize how hard it must be to bear all my financial burdens. But I just feel so powerless when it comes to accomplishing my goals. Sometimes it is hard for me to just get out of bed. Every day now I pray to God to lift my depression. There are so many things that at the moment feel unattainable—a driver's license, college, a job, and one day maybe a family.

The fact is that in the future I may face an even bigger challenge. My addiction to DXM is beatable, but what about other Pandora's boxes yet to be opened? I fear that there may come a time when these days will seem like a blissful memory. But for now, I just wanted you to know that I love you, and I cannot fathom how much you care about your family. But if in the future my life is past redemption, if I should come into contact with greater forces, I do not wish for you to carry the burden of my life on your shoulders.

This letter to you is to show you that I do notice how much you sacrifice for me. I mean, the hours you put in daily to get me to where I need to go are astonishing. The money you have spent, and all the time you have given just to visit me all the times I have been away. The trips to rehabs, and numerous hospital visits. I truly believe that God will bless you for your kindness. And as I fight to provide a better future for myself, I sincerely hope that one day I will be a man you can be proud to proclaim as your son. I am a shell of a man, please don't try to tell me that this is something you are proud of. I have no accomplishments, and I have gained nothing. As I grow to be more mature and try to make responsible decisions, I have learned how to feel the pain that others go through. As I myself am beat down by depression, I feel how others suffer as well. That is why I am expressing my wish for you, Mom. If I should succeed this time in my recovery, and I am feeling fairly certain that my ordeal with DXM has come to an end, then you may rejoice in the fact that, without you, none of my recovery, my very existence would have been possible.

But if I should be nineteen, or twenty, and still failing, I want you to live for your family, Nicole, Alex, Rudy, and Peter. I cannot take up all your time, as there are others who need you. Hopefully I will be a man you can be proud of, but I hope never to be the bane of anyone's existence.

And so it is with this letter I thank you, for the selfless love you have shown me.

Your son,
Daniel

(circa 2009)

CHAPTER 9

Looking Ahead

When Daniel first started falling apart, so did I. I couldn't take care of myself. I couldn't do my hair or get dressed or go to the gym—some days I couldn't get out of bed. I ate horribly and I had to take a sleeping pill to get to sleep. I was so scared all the time that I just kept my hands over my ears and let myself go. My stress level was through the roof thinking about what could be happening to Daniel, and my guilt level was through the roof thinking about having to leave Alexander to go deal with another crisis. The fear and the guilt haven't gone away, but a lot of things are different now.

I've learned that I don't need to get involved in every fight and that I need to be more protective of myself and my time. For a long time, when anyone called asking me to speak at a meeting, or help them find a treatment center, I would immediately drop everything and make a thousand calls to make it happen. I started TAM and stayed up all night to take care of other people's children when I felt I couldn't take care of my own. But I've realized now that the truth is, TAM is so much bigger than me. It's something I started, and I'm incredibly proud of that, but it has grown to become a community of thousands and thousands of moms, and others, who used to be sitting in the dark, desperate and alone. Now they have each other. Now they're sisters—strangers who have become a family. Sometimes we disagree, but we are all the same in the way it counts. Every day, a TAM mom helps someone else's kids find treatment, writes a letter to a judge in support of someone else's child, visits someone else's child in jail, and supports someone who used to have no one who could understand them. Every day we hear stories of children who have achieved recovery after years of feeling hopeless. And the horrible reality is, every day on TAM another child dies. Sometimes more than one child. But at least I know there are always others there to do for that child's parents what so many people did for me, and that is something I can be truly proud of.

I'm different now. I'm older and sadder and feel the weight of so much time I missed with my family. But for the first time since this all started, I've been able to meet with a group of women and not be the leader. I can go somewhere and not be "The Addict's Mom." I've met a bunch of other women in my neighborhood, and I can just get together with them to play canasta and never even mention addiction. I've learned that I don't have to try to save the world anymore.

I swim almost every day. We have a pool at our house, and I think I only used it once while Daniel was alive. I used to avoid going outside for very long because I would get sunburnt, but I decided that swimming is now essential to my life, so I built a big screen over the pool. Now, I'll spend two hours out there just exercising and listening to music, and I won't let anyone bother me. I eat a lot better. I've never really liked drinking, but now I won't even touch alcohol, and Rudy doesn't either.

In the moments when I'm really scared, I'll hang out with Rudy, and I'll hug him. Rudy went from being single at thirty-five with no kids, to having three kids, and then four. And then he went through eight years fighting with me about his addicted stepsons. I have seen the physical toll all of this took on him, and there were several times we didn't think we would survive it, together or apart. After Daniel died, Rudy and I both knew we had to make a choice. We either had to forgive each other or leave each other, and we decided to forgive. We will never agree on how we should or should not have handled many things in the past. But at the end of the day, we love each other. We are so kind to each other now, and I hold his hand and tell him I love him every chance I get. It's a blessing to love someone that much and have them love you back.

Peter, Nicole, and Alex are all doing great. That's unsurprising since they are all such beautiful and intelligent people, but given everything they've been through, it's amazing all the same. Nicole is like my best friend. We talk every day and see each other all the time. She was the youngest graduate in her class at her PA school and already has an amazing career. I'll brag about her every chance I can.

Alex also amazes me and has grown into such a beautiful young man. He's going to college and, at eighteen, has his own business detailing cars. If you can believe it, Rudy raised him to be so responsible that he insists on paying his own car insurance, so he gives us money for that every month. I love hanging out with him and helping him study and watching him grow up.

And I'm much closer to Peter. We talk regularly now. I have done my best to apologize and start to make amends with Peter. I knew better than to let him be where he was, and I wish I would have been strong enough to protect him from everything he's been through. I wish I would have gotten out of my own head and recognized how much he needed me when he was still so vulnerable. I know we still have a lot of work to do on our relationship, but I really want to do it. We have both come such a long way, and I'm so proud of all the work he has put into himself and his recovery. His very existence gives me the comfort and happiness of knowing I had a child who fought addiction and adversity and won. His hard work has truly paid off, and he is doing better than I could have hoped for.

My main goal right now in life is to spend as much good, fun, quality time with my family as I can. Getting to know them, loving them, and refocusing on what is good in my life. My family, and the simple things that make me happy, have to come first. I'm really so lucky to have all of them. I guess you have to have luck somewhere, right?

My other goal is to work on forgiving myself, which is not easy to do. I know I have to try, because that's one of the most important things Daniel taught me. I know everyone remembers different parts of him, and, for some, his words and actions in his darkest times are what stand out the most. But I knew the true Daniel, and he was the nicest, most forgiving person I have ever met. He would stay up all night bringing water to the homeless. He was always willing to share everything he had with me, with other moms, and with anyone who needed it. When someone would fall while beating him up, he would reach out to help them up. He was incredible, and he always encouraged me to forgive. I will never truly heal from losing my son, but I want to honor him now by treating myself and my family right and doing good for the world. Outside of me, he will always live on through the legacy he left in his writing and in TAM and in the people who knew him.

I also know now that I was not honoring Daniel by destroying myself and letting my family suffer while he was alive. When your child is experiencing the horror of addiction, your whole life flashes by and you don't live it at all. You discount that you're the child of somebody. You discount your family. You discount the importance of your own life, your career goals. You discount everything about yourself. The message I want to give to every addict's mom is that while you're so involved in your addict's life, you're not honoring your own life. I can pick an addict's mom out from her picture. She looks so sad and disheveled, and I can tell she's sacrificing her money and her marriage and herself. Sometimes honoring your child means realizing that they have a disease and you can't always save them. Sometimes you have to let go of control. I never could do that. I used to sign my letters "Daniel's Mom," and that's part of who I am, but I'm also so much more than that. I'm Barbara.

In 2016, I was invited to Washington, D.C., to represent my work with TAM and receive the honor of a Champions of Change award from President Obama. I was recommended for the award by former Recovery Czar Michael Botticelli, who joined TAM in an effort to fully understand the widespread effects of addiction on families. To tell the truth, I didn't even want to go. At that time, I was so destroyed by Daniel's death, I couldn't bring myself to do much of anything. But I knew how huge the opportunity was: for me, for Daniel's story, and for every other mother out there like me, so I went, and my whole family went with me. When I had a chance to speak, I shared the biggest lesson I found in all of this:

> I lost my son over a year ago. I didn't know that I would lose a child, but I did know that there had to be thousands, tens of thousands, if not millions of mothers across this country just like me who didn't know where to turn. I want every mother who's an addict's mom to understand that you matter, that you're important. I'm not only an addict's mom. I'm Rudy's wife, I'm Peter's mother, I'm Alex's mother, I'm Nicole's mother, I'm a friend, I'm a cousin, I'm a neighbor. I matter. And if you're an addict's mom, you matter. And whether your child is going through this horrible disease of addiction, whether they're getting better or they're not, it's important that you take care of yourself. You're not alone. I'm an addict's mom, and I'm not ashamed.

Recommended Resources

Addiction barrages us with questions: How do I get my child into treatment? How can I support their recovery? How can I support myself? These resources provide answers to every recovery question you might have and prepare you for a winning battle.

Addict in the Family
Stories of Loss, Hope, and Recovery
by Beverly Conyers

Family stories of addiction that provide lessons and encouragement for families with an addicted loved one.

(Hazelden Publishing, Order No. 1018)

Everything Changes
Help for Families of Newly Recovering Addicts
by Beverly Conyers

This book guides us through the emotional early stages of a loved one's recovery and shows why healthy expectations, support, and boundaries are essential.

(Hazelden Publishing, Order No. 3807)

In the Realm of Hungry Ghosts
Close Encounters with Addiction
by Gabor Maté, MD

In a completely reimagined understanding of addiction, Dr. Gabor Maté leverages his twenty years spent treating addicts on the streets of Vancouver to provide us with a clear and modern interpretation of addiction and why it manifests.

(North Atlantic Books)

It Takes a Family
A Cooperative Approach to Lasting Sobriety
by Debra Jay

Debra Jay teaches us how to create a structured model of family support and collaboration so every member can become a loving part of the recovery team. (Hazelden Publishing, Order No. 7559)

Not by Chance
How Parents Boost Their Teen's Success In and After Treatment
by Tim Thayne

Therapist and residential treatment professional Tim Thayne highlights the ways in which a young person's healthy recovery is sabotaged and how we, as a family, can encourage, instead of prevent, long-term sobriety. (Advantage Media Group)

Recovering My Kid
Parenting Young Adults in Treatment and Beyond
by Joseph Lee, MD

Dr. Joseph Lee teaches us how to rebuild our family and our trust in our addicted child, and rally our family around the child's needs and recovery. (Hazelden Publishing, Order No. 4693)

MEMOIR

You are never alone. Whatever pain you feel, someone else feels too. The voices and victims of addiction are many. These memoirs each tell personal stories of family loss and healing, from which we may all learn and find comfort.

Beautiful Boy
A Father's Journey Through His Son's Addiction
by David Sheff

In this *New York Times* best seller, a helpless father tries desperately to save his beautiful boy before addiction steals him away forever. (Mariner Books)

The Joey Song
A Mother's Story of Her Son's Addiction
by Sandra Swenson

Author Sandra Swenson learns what it means to let go and find her own peace while her beloved, addicted child refuses all of her attempts to help him get sober.

(Central Recovery Press, LLC)

Mothering Addiction
A Parent's Story of Heartache, Healing, and Keeping the Door Open
by Lynda Harrison Hatcher

Lynda Harrison Hatcher shares the honest pains that result from having a son addicted to heroin and what that journey taught her about her own mental health and self-care.

(Frontier Press)

Saving Jake
When Addiction Hits Home
by D'Anne Burwell

Winner of the 2016 Eric Hoffer Book Award in Memoir, D'Anne Burwell brings us inside a home ravaged by addiction. We see addiction tear the Burwell family apart by the seams while Jake races toward a seemingly inevitable catastrophe.

(FocusUp Books)

Tweak
Growing Up on Methamphetamines
by Nic Sheff

For those looking to learn more about the experiences of an addicted child, this *New York Times* best seller by Nic Sheff, the son of *Beautiful Boy* author David Sheff, is a must-read. Nic shares his experiences in the dark reality of addiction and how, eventually, he is able to escape its death sentence.

(Atheneum Books for Young Readers)

A Very Fine House
A Mother's Story of Love, Faith, and Crystal Meth
by Barbara Cofer Stoefen

Author Barbara Cofer Stoefen learns how to save herself while she battles against her daughter's untiring cycle of meth addiction.

(Zondervan)

MEDITATION AND HEALING

Our love for our children will never end. Our lives have centered around their needs since the very start. Using these resources, it's now time to start giving some of our love and comfort back to ourselves.

Codependent No More
How to Stop Controlling Others and Start Caring for Yourself
by Melody Beattie

For those of us who struggle with healthy boundaries, this classic, best-selling book by Melody Beattie teaches us how to stop compromising our own needs and start looking out for our own health and wellness.

(Hazelden Publishing, Order No. 5014)

Conquering Shame and Codependency
8 Steps to Freeing the True You
by Darlene Lancer

For those of us healing from an unhealthy marriage or relationship with an addicted person, Darlene Lancer provides eight actionable steps for overcoming both shame and codependency, helping us to find healthy love and live our best lives.

(Hazelden Publishing, Order No. 7554)

Find Your Light
Practicing Mindfulness to Recover from Anything
by Beverly Conyers

Recovery and wellness expert Beverly Conyers explains why mindfulness is an irreplaceable part of our health and healing toolkit. Whether we are recovering from addiction, codependency, anxiety, disordered eating, or any other behavioral or emotional health issue, this approachable book can help us illuminate the best parts of ourselves. For more mindfulness practice, also look for the follow-up guided journal, *Follow Your Light.*
(Hazelden Publishing, Order No. 3591)

The Grief Club
The Secret to Getting Through All Kinds of Change
by Melody Beattie

Having lost a child of her own, Melody Beattie understands too well the pain of a suffering parent. She channels her experiences and deft writing to gift us a deeply impactful book that helps us move forward from any kind of loss.
(Hazelden Publishing, Order No. 2606)

The Language of Letting Go
Daily Meditations on Codependency
by Melody Beattie

In a convenient daily-reader format, Melody provides us once again with the words and thoughts we need to keep healthy boundaries around our needs and ensure each day is lived to its fullest.
(Hazelden Publishing, Order No. 5076)

A Life of My Own
Meditations on Hope and Acceptance
by Karen Casey

By beloved recovery author Karen Casey, this book of daily meditations helps the loved ones of addicts shift the focus back toward themselves. Inspirational and affirming, each word will give us the strength to heal and grow.
(Hazelden Publishing, Order No. 1070)

Tending Dandelions

Honest Meditations for Mothers with Addicted Children

by Sandra Swenson

In this meditation book created specifically for mothers of addicted children, Sandra Swenson channels her own experiences into a cathartic source of strength and relief for other mothers to rely upon each day.

(Hazelden Publishing, Order No. 3481)

ONLINE RESOURCES

Visit these helpful websites for more valuable information on addiction, mental health disorders, treatment, and recovery, and to join support communities that prove you are not alone.

> Addictsmom.com
>
> Al-anon.org
>
> Drugabuse.gov
>
> Drugfree.org
>
> Hazeldenbettyford.org
>
> Mompower.org
>
> NAMI.org
>
> Nar-anon.org
>
> Palgroup.org
>
> Recoveryanswers.org
>
> Samhsa.gov
>
> SMARTrecovery.org

Acknowledgments

In early 2014, my father was in the hospital. He ended up living for more than a year after that, but he was very sick and we weren't sure how long he had left. I called him and after chatting for a few minutes, out of nowhere, he said, "Barbara, I want to tell you something." I said, "What, Dad?" He replied, "Do you know what the greatest words are in the whole world?" I replied, "Dad I am not sure . . . are they 'I love you'?" "No!" he shouted, "They are *thank you*. The greatest words in the whole world are *thank you*. Barbara," he went on, "remember to say 'thank you' to everyone. No matter how little or how much they do, thank them. Every person needs to hear a kind word, especially the words 'thank you.'" Since then, I have made an effort to include the words "thank you" in my daily language as much as possible. I thank him, dearly, for that piece of wisdom and everything he taught me throughout my life, which was a lot. There are countless people to thank for this project and where I am in my life right now, so if I don't include some of them, still know that I am immensely grateful to everyone who has lent a helping hand to myself, Daniel, and my family throughout the years recounted in these pages.

I would like to thank my husband, Rudy, and my children, Peter, Nicole, and Alex. I cannot thank you enough for all of the love, support, time, and emotion that you put into this project. You are truly the embodiment of what it means to share without shame.

To the rest of my family, thank you for helping me become the person I am today. I love you.

To all of my TAM sisters, you do not get enough credit for everything you do to help save lives every single day. You were there for my family and me in our darkest moments, and words cannot express how grateful I am for you.

To Jessica Ward for honoring and representing families everywhere by creating the beautiful TAM quilt shown on the cover and end pages of this book.

To John Lavitt, who beautifully told Daniel's story on *The Fix* and then worked many hours to help my family and me process and tell our stories. Thank you, truly. You serve as a daily example that recovery is possible.

Thank you to the editors and staff at Hazelden Publishing who made this book possible. My sincere gratitude to Heather Silsbee, Christian Johnson, Terri Kinne, Jean Cook, Don Freeman, Sara Perfetti, Wendy Videen, Chris Deets, Jill Grindahl, and everyone else who contributed to this book along the way.

Finally, to Daniel. I believe you taught me more than I taught you. You are my light and constant inspiration. Thank you for helping me share our story, and the stories of countless other families.

■

About the Author

Barbara Theodosiou is a mother, an activist, and the founder of The Addict's Mom, an online community where tens of thousands of mothers of addicted children can "Share Without Shame." Barbara has been widely recognized for her work as a family recovery advocate, including the receipt of a White House Champions of Change award in 2016.

She is also the author of the action-oriented follow-up to this book titled *Living Without Shame: A Support Book for Mothers with Addicted Children*. While Barbara is proud of the spotlight she's been able to shine on addiction's impact on families, she is most proud of her roles as a daughter, wife, sister, mother, and friend.

You can join The Addict's Mom community by visiting addictsmom .com or joining The Addict's Mom closed group on Facebook.

Take the next step on your healing journey with . . .

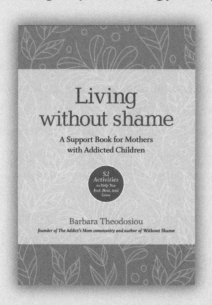

Living Without Shame

A SUPPORT BOOK FOR MOTHERS WITH ADDICTED CHILDREN

52 Activities to Help You Feel, Heal, and Grow

by Barbara Theodosiou

• • •

As a fellow mom, Barbara's message to you is that you matter, regardless of what is happening with the addicted loved ones in your family. Now it's time to take the next step in your own recovery. The exercises in this beautiful, full-color support book are designed to help you take a few minutes each week to feel your feelings, heal from your past experiences, and grow into an even stronger, healthier woman and mom.

Look for *Living Without Shame* at a bookstore near you
or order directly from Hazelden Publishing at
hazelden.org/bookstore.

Take Pride

When my kids were little, it wasn't always easy for us. At one point I was a single mom with three children. It often felt like we were doing nothing but surviving. When we would spend time together at the beginning or end of each day, I often used to ask my kids to tell me things that they had done that day that made them proud. It helped us feel more like we were thriving rather than just surviving.

At the peak of my sons' addictions, when I felt myself becoming little more than "the addict's mom," I found myself in survival mode again. I ceased being me. I stopped living.

By taking pride in ourselves, our actions, and our day-to-day life, we pay attention to ourselves again. We re-emerge as people. We start thriving again.

What are five things you've done or said recently that make you feel proud of yourself?

1.

2.

3.

4.

5.

Sorry, Self

Shame is often accompanied by feelings of low self-worth. That is, sometimes we let the shame other people cast on us take our power because we're already not feeling very powerful, valuable, or worthy. Learning to be gentle with ourselves is a big step forward in feeling a sense of inner peace. Sometimes it feels like we're always apologizing to other people for things we've done or for who we are. When it comes to addiction's impact on a family, we often apologize to those around us for how our loved one's addiction has impacted them. But when was the last time you apologized to yourself?

List five times when you were too hard on yourself, expected too much of yourself, thought too little of yourself, allowed someone to push you too far, or generally mistreated yourself. Then say, "Sorry, self!"

1.

2.

3.

4.

5.

The biggest paradox:
To be happy, surrender to what hurts.
Forgiveness isn't a one-time deal.
The need to make peace is ongoing.

~ Melody Beattie

Climb Every Mountain

...e faced with your child's addiction have likely been
... of your life; however, your child's addiction is
...ribe the story of the "steepest" mountain you've
...llenge you have surmounted. How do you think
...p others?

Tell the story of the mountain you climbed.
Your words could become a page
in someone else's survival guide.
—Morgan Harper Nichols

Overcome

About Hazelden Publishing

As part of the Hazelden Betty Ford Foundation, Hazelden Publishing offers both cutting-edge educational resources and inspirational books. Our print and digital works help guide individuals in treatment and recovery, and their loved ones. Professionals who work to prevent and treat addiction also turn to Hazelden Publishing for evidence-based curricula, digital content solutions, and videos for use in schools, treatment programs, correctional programs, and electronic health records systems. We also offer training for implementation of our curricula.

Through published and digital works, Hazelden Publishing extends the reach of healing and hope to individuals, families, and communities affected by addiction and related issues.

For more information about Hazelden publications,
please call **800-328-9000**
or visit us online at **hazelden.org/bookstore**.

Other Titles That May Interest You

The Grandfamily Guidebook
Wisdom and Support for Grandparents Raising Grandchildren
Andrew Adesman, MD, and Christine Adamec

Are you, or someone you know, one of the nearly three million grandparents across North America raising your grandchildren? In this invaluable and practical guidebook you'll find expert medical advice, helpful insights gleaned from other grandparents like you, tips on how to cope with difficult birth parents and school issues, and strategies for focusing on your own self-care.
Order No. 3620; also available as an ebook

Readings for Moms of Addicts
Sandra Swenson

As a follow-up to her beloved meditation book, *Tending Dandelions,* Sandy Swenson has released this mobile app with 146 new, honest readings that mothers can carry with them wherever they go.
Available on the Apple App Store and Google Play

Blackout Girl
Growing Up and Drying Out in America
Jennifer Storm

Soon to be a made into a documentary film with the same name, this tender and gritty memoir explores Jennifer Storm's childhood history of addiction, sexual assault, and trauma. In a story filled with honesty and hope against all odds, Storm reveals how she was ultimately able to heal from her past and devote her life to helping other victims.
Order No. 9926; also available as an ebook.

Hazelden Publishing books are available at fine bookstores everywhere.
To order from Hazelden Publishing,
call **800-328-9000** or visit **hazelden.org/bookstore.**

family photos

Peter, Nicole, Alexander, and Daniel in 2009

If we can share our story with someone
who responds with empathy and
understanding, shame can't survive.

—BRENÉ BROWN

Nicole, Barbara, and Daniel

Nicole, Rudy, and Daniel

Daniel, Peter, and baby Nicole
at Christmastime

*Barbara with her father, Leon,
and young Peter*

*Nicole as a toddler with her grandparents,
Beverly and Leon*

Rudy, Barbara, and baby Alexander

"Blue Mommy and Blue Peter," painted by Peter when he was four years old

Peter

Alexander and Daniel

Daniel

Barbara and Alexander

Barbara and Rudy

*Alexander dressed for
Homecoming in 2016*

Barbara and Daniel in May 2012

*Barbara and Nicole at Nicole's white coat
ceremony in August 2015*

*Barbara and Rudy at the White House
for the Champions of Change ceremony
in April 2016. Barbara was honored
with the award for her work advancing
addiction prevention, treatment, and
recovery through The Addict's Mom.*